ACCLAIM FOR FREDDIE MAE BAXTER's

The Seventh Child

"At a time when so many memoirs are filled with the narcissistic look-how-I've-suffered neuroses of oh-so-sensitive intellectuals, Ms. Baxter's book reminds that an honest recounting of an ordinary life can teach us how—and why—to live." —*The Washington Times*

"Here is an ordinary woman born black and poor, living in difficult times, who lets us know that although poverty, racism and adverse circumstances do affect us throughout our lives, they must not be allowed to defeat us, as they did not defeat her."
—*The News and Observer*

"Baxter has a good head that took her through some tough experiences. We're lucky to be able to read about her." —*Milwaukee Journal Sentinel*

"Entertaining, enlightening, enriching—*The Seventh Child* is worth your time. Freddie Mae Baxter gives life a fresh perspective." —*Journal Star*, Lincoln, NE

"A beautifully structured and crafted oral history of a woman whose life is both unique and representative. . . . Freddie Mae Baxter's stories, peppered with a homespun philosophy, are acute observations of the passing human comedy." —*New Mexican*, Santa Fe, NM

FREDDIE MAE BAXTER

The Seventh Child

Freddie Mae Baxter lives in Harlem.

The Seventh Child

The Seventh Child

A LUCKY LIFE

FREDDIE MAE BAXTER

Edited by Gloria Bley Miller

VINTAGE BOOKS

A Division of Random House, Inc.

New York

Frontispiece: The Baxter family
Back row, left to right: Daisy, Freddie Mae, Victoria, Margaret
Front row: Henry (Buck), Willie (Bill), Julius

FIRST VINTAGE BOOKS EDITION, MAY 2000

The Library of Congress has cataloged the Knopf edition as follows:
Baxter, Freddie Mae.
The seventh child : a lucky life / by Freddie Mae Baxter. — 1st. ed.
p. cm.
ISBN 0-375-40620-4
1. Baxter, Freddie Mae. 2. Harlem (New York, N.Y.)—
Biography. 3. Afro-American women—New York (State)—New
York—Biography. 4. Afro-Americans—New York (State)—
New York—Biography. 5. Denmark (S.C.)—Biography. 6. Afro-
American women—South Carolina—Denmark—Biography. I. Title.
F128.68.H3B39 1999
974.7'104'092—dc21 [B] 98-54109
CIP

Vintage ISBN: 0-375-70593-7

www.vintagebooks.com

Printed in the United States of America
10 9 8 7 6 5 4 3 2 1

For my mother,
Julia Free Baxter,
who kept us all together

CONTENTS

Editor's Note ix

Growing Up 3

Sisters and Brothers 32

Money and Gambling 51

Coming North 62

God in My Heart 85

Keeping Up with the Dead 95

"Stardust" Was Special 108

Working 117

Children 141

Women and Men 151

Friends 171

Harlem 199

My Day 208

Having Fun 218

A Lucky Life 222

I first met Freddie Mae Baxter some twenty years ago when she was working as a cook and housekeeper for a friend of mine, who was then in her seventies. Whenever I visited, Freddie Mae and I would just say hello and goodbye. Sometimes we'd talk about the weather.

On reaching her nineties, my friend broke her hip and went to an out-of-town nursing home. Freddie Mae phoned and asked if I'd like to accompany her there since she knew the way. We arranged to meet on the train. I'd get on at Grand Central Station and she at 125th Street in Harlem, where she lived.

Sitting side-by-side on the train during the hour-long ride, we talked about ourselves and our lives, speaking with each other as if for the very first time. I was enchanted by Freddie Mae's way of looking at the world, by her warmth and great humor.

In the months that followed, we traveled together to the nursing home half a dozen times or so. When I talked to Freddie Mae about her childhood and her family, I discovered what a fine storyteller she was, and I was struck by the idea of putting it all down on paper. When I first suggested this to Freddie Mae, she was a bit dubious. But when I brought it up again, she decided she had nothing to lose by trying it.

We met at my apartment every Friday afternoon. We sat in the living room with a small tape recorder on a little table between us. The tape ran 45 minutes on each side. When the second side ran out, the session had ended.

For twenty years, Freddie Mae had been someone I only said héllo to. Then everything changed. In the year it took us to put this book together, we became two people who could really talk to each other. Freddie Mae Baxter has now told her story in her own words, with its own shapes and its own rhythms. And I have done my best to write it all down.

Gloria Bley Miller

The Seventh Child

GROWING UP

I grew up in a town called Denmark, South Carolina—like Denmark in that other country. It was a pretty big place then and is a very big place now, but I can't tell you how many people live there. My mother and father were married and my mother's name was Julia and my father's name was Henry. They had eight kids: five girls and three boys. My mother told me she was pregnant with me when my grandma died. I don't know anything about my grandparents, except I think they died in about 1922.

The eldest sister was Lumisha. She was four or five years older than Willie, my oldest brother. He was three to four years older than the next brother, who was Henry. That brother was about two years older than Daisy, the next sister. And Victoria, the next sister, I would say was two and a half years younger than Daisy. Then comes Margaret, who is two years older than me. Then there's me. So that's the five girls. My brother Julius, he's the baby. I'm five years older than Julius. That makes me the seventh child—the lucky one.

My father left when I had to be about five or six. He was supposed to be the father of all the kids but I wouldn't know about that. I really don't know too much about him. I don't know the reason why he left. I don't know how it happened.

My mother didn't give a reason. She didn't say why he left. Nobody asked no questions then and they didn't get no answers. In those days you didn't ask questions. If you tried, they'd say, "Get out of here." And that was it. Children today can ask their momma anything.

I knew my father was in another town after he left my mother. He was the boss of his own farm. He grew everything: corn, cotton, potatoes, tomatoes. He had everything a farm had: horses and mules and plows. My brother Willie went up and helped him one year. But I still didn't ask no questions about him. I was really angry at my father for a long time because all through the years he never got in touch with us. He was doing pretty well but he didn't do anything about his own kids. I heard that he had a lady friend but I never knew for him to have any more children.

My father was the one that I don't think I would've given a piece of bread to if I had a piece of bread. When I used to sit and think about it, I'd say, "How could he? How in the hell could he?" That's all I could say. Now, when you see these TV talk shows where the father leaves the family, I really want to hear everything about it because I don't see how he could've done it.

A father is not like a mother. He walks away and those kids will care more about that father that walked away than they care about the mother that stayed there. That's what I can't understand. On the talk shows, they tell the mother that it's her fault that the father walked away. He can walk away any-time he gets ready. And then he can walk back in there. They seem to care more about that father; they still want to say, "Daddy, Daddy." But if the mother walks away, she's a no-good. I can't understand that. The man is just as involved in the pregnancy as she is. So why does he have to be the one that can walk away and come back and get all that loving? What makes me mad is if a man gives the woman one child or two or three children and he didn't take care of them, how can she have another one for him? If he didn't take care of the three she's already got, how do you think he's going to take care of the fourth one?

When my father left, he went about his business and he stayed about his business. I wouldn't have tried to look for him. I wouldn't have tried to find out if he was sick or whether he died or what happened to him. Because he wasn't there for me. And nobody could say, "Well, he is your father." I wouldn't accept it. But if he had stayed and did for me, I would've walked through fire for him. That's the way I am. They say that blood is thicker than water, but not with me. It might be thicker than water but I could not accept what he did.

For a long time I kept in my mind everything that I had against my father. Then I changed my mind; I just got over it. As I see things of those days, I didn't like my father because I didn't know anything about him. You think back. You don't know what made him walk away. There's always two sides to a story and he wasn't there to tell his side and Momma didn't tell her side. I started seeing things more clearly when I got to be about in my forties. I decided I would get it off my mind; you can destroy yourself if you keep something on your mind like that. Hate can destroy you. You got to give it up. You have to cool it because nobody can do it for you. So I forgave my father.

Back then I didn't talk about how I felt with my brothers and sisters. I never spoke to anyone in the family about it except Margaret. (She had to be about seven when he left.) I said to her, "You know I've been wondering why Poppa left and I really did resent it when he left. I just wanted him around." And I said to Margaret, "What about you? How do you feel about Poppa, like we grew up without him and everything?" And she said, "It didn't make any difference to me. I never felt any kind of way. I never did feel like he was there." And she said, "He wasn't there. He just wasn't there. I never thought about him."

That's the kind of person Margaret is. She really don't care. She says she don't even think about it. We spoke about it just that one time. She answered my question and I had no reason to push her anymore. If she had said, "I kind of thought about that," then I would've had something to build on. Like if I say "Good morning" to you and you say "Good morning" back, I ain't got nothing to build on. You go about your business and I go about mine. I'm not going to bother you if I say "Good morning" and all you say is "Good morning" back.

My mother was very poor. She had eight kids to raise and she didn't have a husband. It seemed like she be thinking all the time. You know how you see a person thinking about something but you never did know about it because in those days they didn't tell you nothing. If they were worried about something, you didn't know it. If they were happy about something, you could kind of see that. But they didn't tell you anything.

My mother wasn't a well-educated person but she was bright. She knew what to tell us to do and how to do it and when to do it. She could tell us about things you should do and shouldn't do. Or what you should eat and what you shouldn't eat. Some of the things she used to tell us you can sometimes read in books right today.

My mother really worked hard to raise us kids together after my father left. She didn't give anybody up. It was very hard for her. She could've given some of us away. But nobody was put off here or put off there. Even Julius, who was the youngest child, he stayed right there until my mother died. She did so much for us by herself. God knows I loved that woman. God knows I did.

I didn't want to grow up. I was like Peter Pan. The other girls in the family, they wanted to go out and visit their girl-friends. But I wanted to be with my momma. I used to stick to her. She worked in service, and after school, I'd go to where she was at. Sometimes the lady she was working for would want me to help her bathe the kids or something like that. I was helping my momma. That lady paid my momma. She wasn't going to pay me. Maybe she'd give me a nickel or something like that. And then when my momma get ready to come home, I'd come home with her. In the night when the other girls were having fun, me and my mother were someplace together. I just wanted to be with my momma.

When my mother had her children, she wanted all of them to be children, not boys and girls. Everybody could do the same thing. There wasn't no such thing as a boy job or a girl job. The boys had to do just what the girls did. And I liked her for that. She didn't say, "All right now, you boys cut the wood and you girls go and make up the beds." It didn't matter if it was a girl that cut the wood or a boy that cut the wood. Or the boy that made the bed or the girl that made the bed. Every one of my brothers could cook a meal, take care of their wife and their children, just like any woman; like they could put on diapers, comb the baby's hair. They could wash, iron, sew, cook. They could do everything for themselves. Every last one of Momma's children could do that. If they didn't want to get married, they didn't have to get married, because they could do everything for themselves.

My mother told us this: Whatever you have, you make sure it's clean. My mother said some kids have three or four dresses but if you have just one dress, and if your one is standing out nice and clean and your skin is clean, you can beat out the others with three or four dresses because they are no cleaner than you are with one. That's why when I see a dirty person, I get angry. Saturday nights was our best time. I used to call Saturday and Sunday "colored people's days." You wasn't working then and you could get yourself together. Them boys would get their shirts clean: They would wash and starch and iron those shirts and go to see the little girls. Now I always say: Whatever you got, if you keep it clean, nobody don't know if you bought it yesterday, twenty years ago, or thirty years ago.

Whatever we had in our house, we would cook it and everybody would sit down together at the table. You put food on the table and you had to say grace before you ate it. And sometimes my mother would come with some more food. She would be working for the families and they have food left over. Sometimes she would come in with half of this and half of that that they didn't eat, because they didn't want no leftovers. Whatever they had that day, they didn't want for tomorrow. So my mother would bring it home and we would serve that too. What little food we had—it wasn't much, but we had enough.

Whatever we had we shared. It was eight of us so if there was food, everybody got a certain amount. It wasn't like you could go back and say, "I want some more." So you shared it. We didn't have anything to fight about because we didn't have anything. We were poor but we didn't have a bad life. You know you can have and not be happy and you can not have and be happy. We just didn't have anything but we were happy. What we had, we ate and that was it.

If there was a piece of bread, we all shared that piece of bread together. Because nobody is gonna eat it all by themselves, they gonna fix it so somebody else gets some. If you didn't share, my mother would say something like, "You know you got enough there. You give her some." It's almost like a tree. You have a little tree and you bend it when it's small but you can't bend it after it grows up. Even if you ain't got nothing, if you got love you can almost produce something. But when you don't love, you can't share. In my family, we were taught to love. We were taught to take care of each other and love each other. We didn't have anything but we had lots of love.

For our big meal of the day, we'd eat peas and rice and beans and cornbread. We had meat. We wasn't no vegetarians.

We had pigs. Way back then, we had two or three pigs killed a year around Thanksgiving and in the wintertime. We had chickens. We had plenty of vegetables. If you make a garden, you have all the vegetables that you want.

Look at how we grew up. We didn't have all that stuff that they say you got to have, like vitamins. We didn't know anything about it. And there wasn't such a thing as what's good for you and what's bad for you. Now this is my theory—I'm not saying it's right but I'm thinking for me—if you're someplace where you can't get no food, you can eat anything and it will not hurt you. But when you get where they say, "Oh, this is not good for you and that is not good for you," you get it in your mind that if you eat it, it's gonna kill you.

The only time we got all kinds of fruit was at Christmas. Every child in the family would get one orange, one banana, one apple, and some nuts. My mother had a little place set up at Christmas where each child's stuff was. Sometimes you'd even get a big round coconut! The only fresh fruit you had the rest of the year was like if you had a peach tree, a pear tree, or an apple tree in your yard. We had a plumgranate tree in our yard. (A plumgranate is a big red thing that burst open with little seeds.) Fruit wasn't something you went to the store to buy, except at Christmas.

Every once in a while my mother could buy a little something. It wouldn't be big, just something to know you had a little something new for Christmas. The nuts we got at Christmastime would be from our pecan tree. I had to be about eleven when I started thinking about it. "Now wait a minute," I said. I asked my mother, "How come Santa Claus know how to give us nuts just like off our tree?" and "How does Santa Claus come and bring us the little toys that we got?" I figured it out that some white family my mother was working for would give her a doll and other things that their kids had played with and that she'd bring those toys home.

When I found out there was no Santa Claus, that was the

end of Christmas for me. As long as you let a kid feel there's a Santa Claus and keep with that spirit, Christmas is fine. But the minute he finds out it isn't so, Christmas is just another day.

In my day, there was no making money. You were lucky if you could make seventy-five cents a day. And you couldn't do anything about it because everybody else was making the same. So how could you ask for more if nobody else was making more? Way back then, you could buy two cents worth of anything. Two cents was money in those days. You could buy two cents worth of rice, about two cents worth of sugar, two cents worth of meal. Take rice: For two cents you could get about a cup and a half, a good little bagful. You could even buy two cents worth of bacon. You could take fifteen cents and buy a lot of stuff. You could buy anything with a nickel and a dime. A dime was money. I was rich when I got hold of a dime. If you had two dollars, you'd have to have somebody help you bring home all the stuff you could buy with that. Now two dollars can't buy anything. It would be like twenty dollars today.

One lady my mother worked for—she was a big old fat lady with curly red hair—she used to come and get Momma in her car once a month and they'd go to another town. When they came back that car would be loaded. She would buy Momma everything: meat, sugar, rice, lard, chicken, everything. When that lady pulled up in our yard, we would have to come to the car and help to get our stuff in the house. I'll never forget that lady as long as I live.

You didn't talk back to parents in those days. You know that children gonna talk if their parents do something they don't like or won't let them do something. In those days you could talk but you had better make sure it's under. That means the children could talk within but they couldn't bring it out. You better not say a bad word out loud. If I had talked to my mother like the kids today talk to their parents, I would've been called armless—she would've wrung these arms right out of my shoulders. We didn't talk back to no momma. We would get whippings. It might sound cruel, but I'm so glad she did it. Because if she had let us have our way and do what we wanted to do, all of us could have been jailbirds. I wouldn't be here today.

Today kids get angry and don't talk under, they talk right out. They tell their mothers exactly what they want to tell them. And they do it on the talk shows on TV too. I guess people do it because they want to be on television or something. But I know I wouldn't do it. I think you should keep it to yourself.

In those days, kids had better not raise their hands to hit their parents. Our people would kill you; they would actually kill you. Like you hear some mothers talk on TV shows and say how they're afraid of their kids. Our mothers and fathers were not afraid. All the kids were whipped then. They'd hit those kids on the side of the head. Today they say that if the kids do something wrong, you got to talk to them. But sometimes talking don't do it. If most kids were whipped when they were coming up, things wouldn't be as bad as they are today. But if you wait until they get to be teenagers and all of a sudden you want them to mind you, they're not going to mind you. If you don't bend that branch when it's little, you're not going to bend no tree when it gets grown.

We didn't talk back to Momma. Today a child will say, "Oh, Momma. Shut up and let me talk." Good gracious alive, if we did that, she would hit us with her hand when we said something you're not supposed to say in front of grown people. She would knock us somersault into the fireplace. My mother was short but she wasn't skinny. She was the beatingest little woman I've ever seen in my whole life.

If us kids fought with each other, my mother would beat

everybody. That little woman would whip you and you had to take it. She would use a switch from a tree and plait it like you plait your hair and whip you with it. When we got older, we even had to make our own whip—and there was no saying you wasn't gonna do it. My mother would send me out to the peach tree to get three prongs, three branches. And I'd strip the leaves off there. I used to cry as I stripped the leaves off.

My mother was supposed to beat me to make me do the right thing. She wanted me to know how to grow up and be a woman. She knew I'd just have to get it right the first time. I'm glad for every beating that she gave me, every one. But I used to try to not get them. And if I did do anything, I'd say, "Momma, I love you. I l-o-v-e you, Momma." And I'd hug and kiss her. I was always one of them lovey-doveys. I didn't get whipped very often because I always tried to stay out of the way. I tried to do the right thing but sometimes I would kind of slide back a bit. Maybe the worst thing I ever did was to beat up on my youngest brother, Julius. I got a tail-whipping for that and I never hit him again. I'm really glad about the things my mother made me do because that taught me to be a lady today.

My brothers and sisters, they got whipped. Daisy and Henry would make trouble. They set people against each other. And Margaret got whipped more than anybody: She always just did what she had to do. Momma beat them until they were grown women and men to make sure they didn't fight with each other.

We didn't fight much, but every once in a while you might get a little mixup. (We never really hit or took a stick or tried to cut.) We'd get angry and say things out of the way but not bad enough to hurt each other. But if somebody else out there came along and hit one of your sisters or brothers, then everybody was on him. I got in many fistfights to protect my little brother Julius.

Children should be closer to each other than to their

mother and father because the sisters and brothers were in their mother's belly together. You all were in the same place for nine months. You and your sister or you and your brother should be able to talk together and don't tell it back to the parents. That's one thing in my family, we will always help each other.

I love my brothers and sisters and when I tell you I love, I really love. All of us, we'd really do anything for each other. That's what I call a strong, strong bond. You don't let nobody come in between that. I'll share anything with my brothers and sisters. You let me hit a million dollars on the Lotto, I'm gonna share it with everybody. Because if I don't, I'll put it in the bank and I'm gonna have to keep giving, giving, giving. So I'm gonna share it and everybody will have a little piece.

There are families where people haven't spoken to each other for forty years. You'd be surprised how much energy people waste up. Some of them will say to you, "Momma died and she meant for me to have this or she meant for me to have the other." And the sister, she wanted it all and the brother, he wanted it all so they haven't spoken to each other since Momma died. Ain't no way in the world that I'd stay away from my family on account of something I didn't get that Momma had or something I didn't get that Poppa had. That's material things. You can go to the store and buy that if you want it. And are you going to stay out from your family for twenty or thirty years because you didn't get a blanket or a bedspread or a diamond ring?

When I was a little girl, I always thought I was something but I just didn't have anything to show it off with. Oh, I had long beautiful hair and my coloring wasn't too bad. If only I had something, I really would have been out-of-sight. I didn't have clothes and nice little bows on my hair like some little girls had. I would get so angry I would just want to tear them apart. They used to give these little children birthday parties but they wouldn't invite me because all the children had to have on nice dresses and I didn't have one. And it used to hurt me. I would see them having these parties: When you're in the South, one house would be over here and one would be over there. You could see what people were doing in the next yard.

The mother would ask the children, "Who do you want to invite?" And they didn't name me even though I played with them all week long in school. I don't blame the children's mothers for not inviting me because if the mother had of made me come and the kids didn't want me, I would have had a dull time. You know children are very cruel. They say things because that's the child in them. They wouldn't do it if they got to be grown and knew that it would hurt you very bad.

So I used to feel very bad about birthday parties. I would try not to let people see me cry. I'd go someplace and sulk for a while. Sometimes I couldn't help but show it. I never had kids but I promised if I ever had some, I never would do that to another kid because I know what it did to me.

I used to play with some children who lived with their grandmother. The real mother was up North and she would come to visit the children and bring them all kinds of toys and clothes. Sometimes I would be there when she came and not one of them would say, "Oh, that little girl over there, I'm gonna give her something too." They never did. And I'd think, "Why can't you give me something? Why? I'm a kid just like your kid. Why hurt me?" 'Cause I was hurt. I don't mean hurt like hitting me. I would rather be hit. I would rather you beat me than hurt my feelings. Beating is over in a period of minutes and then it's gone. But the heart pain is not going anyplace.

And I never forgot that. I promised that if I came to your house and I bought presents for your kids but didn't have enough to go around for the other kids there, those kids would never know it. I'd tell you to put those presents in the closet until after those other kids had gone home and then give them to your kids. Because to see a kid's hurt face, it would really come back to me and hurt me again because that used to hurt me so bad.

When I was a little girl, I was tough but kind. Sometimes you have to fight. When a new person comes to school, he better learn to fight until he can get involved with the other kids. (If you don't fight, then you always get picked on until they get tired of you.) When we were fighting, we didn't hurt nobody like the children you see today, knifing each other. If we fought, it would be strictly a fistfight. We never got a stick. We never got a brick. You had to fight this person until you get him down, until he say, "That's enough."

I fought a lot when I was a kid. The others couldn't give me a hard time because I was like a bully. They couldn't say anything about me. And the boys couldn't do more with me than the girls could. I would hit the boys too. I think I was fighting so much because something was lacking in me. I wanted a family. I wanted my father and mother to be together. And when I saw children that had a mother and father, I beat them up. They got it more than the ones like me, the ones that only had one parent. And the kids that had the birthday parties on Saturday or Sunday, I would get them on Monday morning. I'd say, "You wouldn't invite me to your party." And I'd hit them. I regret it now but a child is a child, you know. I fought enough when I was a kid to never raise my hand to anybody anymore.

Kids hear everything you say. You be talking and you think that because the kids are busy playing, they don't know what you're talking about. But they hear everything. When I was really young, I used to be playing hiding-go-seek with my little friends. I'd be counting one-two-three-four and I'd hear people on the porch saying, "You know, she went out with him." Or "He goes out with So-and-so." And I'd be listening. And they'd say, "She was with him and her husband came there and then she ran and lost her shoe." And I'd be counting five-six-seven-eight and they didn't stop talking. (Sometimes just to make sure they'd think I wasn't paying them no mind, I'd count double.)

Then three or four weeks later when I'd get mad at one of the kids that belonged to this parent, I'd say, "So-and-so ran from your daddy and lost a shoe." So the kid would go home and tell her parents and her mother would tell my mother. When my mother asked me about it, I didn't say that I told those stories because I didn't want to get a beating. I would say, "Oh, no, Momma. I didn't tell her anything." If you said anything about older people, you would get a whipping.

One thing I did that was kind of bad was I told one of my girlfriends that her and another girl were half-sisters. I heard somebody talking about it when I was playing hiding-go-seek. So I told this girl, "I heard that you and So-and-so got the same poppa but not the same momma." (Those two girls really did look alike.) Her momma told my mother what I said. But I said I didn't say it. Do you think I'd want to get whipped when I could say that I didn't say it? It was the other girl's word against mine. Nobody knew whether I heard the story or not. But Momma somehow knew anyway and she tore me completely up. After that, I would never tell that girl anything. She could not even get me to say that the weather was good or bad. After the beating I got then, I promised I'd keep my mouth closed.

Our yard was always full of kids at all times of the day and night, even though we didn't have anything to offer them. We couldn't say to the kids, "Let's go in and get some Kool-Aid." We just was the way we played and the way we loved. The kids that got everything, sometimes they'd say, "We'd like to be Miss Julia's kids" because of the way she raised us and how she always did things with us. Then there would be the mother who if her kid wanted a bike, she would go and buy it for him, and say, go have fun with that bike and leave me alone. Some parents don't try to make a day with their kids, don't have a picnic together or do things with their kids. Not in my family.

We played with different kids. There was this little white boy. His family lived down the road. He was younger than me, the same age as Julius. He used to come up to our house to play and we'd go to his yard to play. His family had a whole yard full of chickens. We didn't have but one chicken, a little bantam rooster. One time he came up to our house to play and he saw this one chicken we had. He said, "Let's chase the chicken." I said, "Chase the chicken? What you mean chase the chicken?" He said, "Oh, you know. We chase at it and he run." And we did it. That chicken, he ran all over the house.

In those days, no house had a basement. Our house was sitting up like on blocks. (We had to sweep under there like we swept the yard.) When the rooster ran up under the house, we could crawl up under there and he'd come out. Then he ran across the field and we were right behind. And we would catch him. We ran that rooster until he got so tired. Then the little white boy said, "Why don't you turn him loose and run him again?" Old stupid me, I said "Okay." So we turned that poor rooster loose and he could hardly make it. (I bet that rooster was saying, "Them mothers . . .") So after a while, that poor rooster conked out and fell over. I said, "Oh, my God! I think he's tired." But that rooster, he fell dead. That little old white boy made us run the chicken until that chicken fell dead. He wanted us to be without any chickens. And he got it so we didn't have any. When our rooster fell dead, that white boy said, "You ain't got any chicken no more."

We didn't tell my mother what happened. We couldn't tell her that we ran our chicken to death. She would've killed us. We said, "Momma, our bantam died. He just died." And that was it. We acted like maybe he ate something. (You know chickens would pick up anything around unless you had them fenced in.) My mother never did find out that we killed that chicken, that we murdered that chicken. I got that secret in me right now.

I was six when I started school. Before that, my mother asked the milkman to go uptown and pick up a little blue book for me. She gave him just a little bit of money for the book, the first book that a child starts reading. I'll never forget the milkman's name. It was Mr. Sim Patrick. Mr. Patrick used to go uptown and get the milk and take it around to different people's houses. When he brought the book back, I started reading it right away, and I read the whole book that same day. I guess I learned to read just hanging around my sisters and brothers; I don't remember exactly how.

The book had a story I never forgot, about a little red hen. This hen wanted to plant some wheat where she could make some bread but nobody would help her. The goats didn't want to help. The cows didn't want to help. Nobody wanted to help. And that really did get to me. I said, "Why couldn't they help her?" But when the wheat got done and she got the bread done and everything, naturally everybody was there with their hand out to get some. When I got to school, the teacher was surprised that I could read the whole book. But she saw that I had learned the whole book, and not by faking it; I knew all the words.

We called the first class the primer—what they now call kindergarten. My first teacher, Miss Bailey, was pretty, with long dark hair: She looked like she could have been a Spanish lady. In those days, we didn't know about Spanish because there were no Spanish people in our town.

In primer, the children used to build with little sticks and things like that and then knock them down. And they'd build, build, build. I told Miss Bailey, "I don't want to build with no sticks. I want to read." When she let me read, I didn't want to stop. So while the other children would be building with sticks, I'd be reading my little book. The only books in the classroom were the same kind of little book I had. When I was promoted from primer to first grade, I was so happy because we finally had some real books.

My first-grade teacher, Esther Jenkins, was real tall. She wasn't pretty. She could play the piano. She had these little sessions where we would read some and then she would teach us how to dance. She would give us programs to do every day. I was good at some of the things like dancing, reciting, and making up my own little stories.

One time I made up a story I recited for the whole first-grade class: "There was this little girl. She didn't have any mother and she didn't have a father." I felt so bad for this little girl that if I ever got grown, I was going to give her all the things her mother and father couldn't give her. Now this wasn't a real true story. I made it all up and stood in front of everybody to tell it, and you know I got an A.

My third-grade teacher was Miss Lorick. Then I went through there with her books. There were higher and higher books each time. We always had to use used books. The white schools got to use the books first, then we would get them for our school, say, the next year. Some of the pages would be torn out or be scratched in but we still learned from them.

The school building I was in had only one story. Primer, first grade, and second grade were in there. You had just one class for first grade, one class for second grade, and one class for third. One teacher had to take care of that whole class of about maybe twenty kids in each room. Then up the road a little bit, there was another building with four rooms in it. That was the fourth grade, fifth grade, sixth grade, and seventh grade. We had to use one room for chapel. We would go there in the morning and say our prayers and sing.

I didn't do badly at school. I studied hard because I never wanted to be where you got to teach me over and over. I'll tell you about math, which we didn't call math then, we called it arithmetic. When we were talking about arithmetic and numbers, I didn't know what it meant at first. So I asked my teacher and she said, "Well, arithmetic means your money. Numbers mean your money." When I found out arithmetic was money, I was the best in the class. Believe it when I tell you. My teacher asked me, "How did you get from down to up?" I told her, "When I found out arithmetic was money, I wanted to count my money. I don't want nobody to count it for me. I can hold any kind of money that belongs to me."

In school, we also studied English, spelling, and geography. Geography and history I think went together. And I remember a class about the presidents. When we got a little further apace, they had more; they had algebra. Now that is something I tried but I could never do.

When I was at school they put on plays but I never was the one that wanted to have the star part of the show. I was mostly in the dance group.

One time—I guess I was in the third or fourth grade—we had a play where the lead song was "My Great-Great-Grandfather Lived Long Ago." A boy sang that. He had on a high top hat and a walking cane. And the girl, she had on a wide hooped skirt and her hair was just so. Her song was "My Great-Great-Grandmother Lived Long Ago." The boy with the tall hat and the girl with the hair, they were supposed to be married. They went on to act just like a grandfather and a grandmother would act. Then they would have a group of girls like sunflowers in yellow with little hats come on and sing. I was one of the sunflowers. There was a little girl who came out like she was a bluebird and she flew all around the stage singing, "Bluebird, bluebird, in my window . . ."

I remember all of them kids that I used to truck around with like that. Some of them were my age. Some were a little younger, some a little older. Of the twenty-five or thirty children that were in my class, only about seven of us are alive today.

· · ·

Fifth grade, that was when the big deal came in. We had a teacher who was a mean old thing but she was one of the best teachers we ever had. Her name was Miss Chapell. I can't say I loved her but I liked the way she made the kids learn. You had to learn with her. You had to know what you were supposed to know if you wanted to be promoted. When you left her class, you were well prepared for the sixth grade. You just didn't pass because you were big or because she liked you or disliked you or because you were bad.

Some kids would stay in the class all year long and probably never get up and answer a question. So Miss Chapell would call on somebody that didn't raise their hand. If you raised your hand all the time, she wouldn't call on you so that's what I did. Sometimes she used to call on me and I did know what the answer was. Sometimes I didn't know it but I'd still raise my hand. That's a chance you got to take. (She didn't catch on to that one.) And she'd call somebody else that didn't raise their hand. Then I said, "Thank God." If she had called on me, maybe I'd have to make up the answer. So I didn't have to work too hard in her class.

But you could not play with Miss Chapell. If you were bad, she would beat you. She had a paddle for that, something like the little thing we had with a rubber ball attached but thicker than that. You had to hold out your hand and she would hit you with the paddle as many times as she thought you did bad or did something to deserve that. And it hurt because she really came down on you. It didn't break nobody's hands or nothing like that. (If it did, I never heard about it.) I got paddled once because I socked a fella. Miss Chapell didn't catch him but she caught me. I said to that fella, "I'm gonna get you later, about five o'clock." And I did.

When you got paddled in school, you didn't go home and tell your parents about it. They wouldn't pay you no mind because they knew you had to do something to deserve it. Because in those days, teachers were honest with the kids. If they said you did something, you did it. Today the teachers will lie and the kids will lie. But when I was going to school down South, the teachers were very honest with the kids.

After you got in the sixth grade and were ready to go to high school, they stopped beating you. They thought you should be a young lady by then and shouldn't do anything to get beat. If you did something you weren't supposed to do, they would talk to you and tell you that you were gonna be expelled. When I finished the tenth grade, that was about the time I left home.

I was a tough little girl. There was a little boy and we'd be out in front of the house dancing, carrying on, and having fun. We were just throwing each other around. I could always throw that boy down. We weren't fighting now, just playing. Cars would pass by and the people in those cars would pull over, come up to us, and give us nickels for me to throw him down again.

You know girls can do just about anything boys can do, like climb a tree. I used to be a tomboy. I played with my brothers a lot. There was only one brother younger than me. The others were older but it didn't make any difference because I thought I was smarter. I could play football just as good as my brothers did. They would sometimes knock me down but I'd get back up. I could play basketball just as good as my brothers, and baseball too.

In school, there was a side for the boys and a side for the girls. The teachers didn't want the boys and girls to play together. Everybody was in the same classroom but you couldn't play together on the outside. I wanted to play with the boys and they even wanted me to be on their team, but the teachers were always on my case. They'd say, "Freddie Mae Baxter, I told you . . ." But I wasn't over there to love the boys. I was over there to play. I used to ease over there, but if the teacher saw you, she would make you go back over to your side.

I was very fast at running. We used to have a Field Day in school. There was a 50-yard dash for the girls and a 100-yard dash for the boys. The 50-yard dash wasn't good for me because I ran too fast and could beat all the girls. There's no good to doing something if you always win. You gotta give somebody else a chance to win too. And I wanted to run the 100-yard dash but that meant I got to be over with the boys. I believe I could have kept up with them, but the teachers didn't like that. I bet I could've beat some of the boys.

I was always making things when I was a kid. I could make a nice slingshot better than any of the boys made. I used the rubber from the inside of car tires and I would cut it into strips. Then I'd take me a limb from a tree and make a little head on each prong with a knife so the rubber you put around there on both sides wouldn't come off. Then I'd get a piece of leather from an old shoe, like a shoe tongue. (That's the thing that's going to hold the rock.) Then I'd shape the piece of leather to be just big enough to put on the rubber. You pull back the rubber and then let go. We'd shoot at rabbits. (We never caught any because a rabbit is real fast. But we'd shoot at them anyway.) We'd hit a bird. We'd shoot at bees, not in the nest, but after they'd fly out. I could make a slingshot so that I could hit almost anything I aimed at.

When my mother brought toys home from the families she worked for, I got many dolls that had been used. But I really liked to make my own dolls. I would take a weed that grew high with a root that is like a lot of strings, turn the root upside down, and the strings would be my doll's hair. Then I would take the green part and fix it up and make little clothes and put little bows on it. And when little children's dolls got broken, I could fix those dolls. You know how the little doll baby has little arms that go in a socket and there's a little piece of something holding them in place? Well, little children were always bringing me their dolls to put the arms back on when they broke off. And I could really fix them. Don't ask me how I did it. I don't know. I guess it's because I'm the seventh child.

I could do a whole lot of things when I was a kid. When I was maybe eleven or twelve, I could use a hammer and I could saw. Nobody had to teach me, because things would come into my mind to do. I made a tree house we could go up to. We used to do a whole lot of things, like play with our dolls. I said to myself that if I could go back there after I got grown, I could get me some lumber and make a bench around the tree we had in the backyard to sit on. And I would plant some grass and different things, and really make me a home.

When I was a kid, the game I loved very much was ring plays. The children would get in a circle and clap their hands and sing songs. I loved the clapping and the singing. Somebody in the middle of the circle would pick someone and bring them there. Then she would go back in the circle. The new person in the middle then got to choose the one she wanted, boy or girl. Boys could play too because that's how you get to love the little boys. (When the boys stop pranking with the girls and you think you're a little grown up, then the girls start getting their little hairbobs and other little things for the boys.)

There were four of us girls; we got a pack, like a gang. In them days, we didn't call it a pack, just four girls. We were getting kinda big, maybe thirteen or fourteen years old. Ruth was the oldest. I was next. Ruby was next and then there was Lily Mae. We used to be devils. We didn't hurt nobody but we sure made them miserable.

We would go someplace and make up a ring play and wait until it got hot. (When I say hot, I mean when everybody was really having fun.) And the children in there, they would choose one of us because they didn't know what we were gonna do. But we wouldn't choose any of them, we just kept choosing each other. That's what you call making them miserable. They all would leave, one by one. Afterward, there would be just the four of us. I don't know why we did it. Like I said, children are cruel but they stop it when they grow up.

I loved those girls even until we got grown. Now all those little girls is gone but me. I'm the only one of the pack that's still here. Two of the girls moved to New York and one was in Washington. I didn't see the Washington one much. Every once in a while, I'd see one of the New York girls but I always kept in touch with the other one. She was married to a very close friend of mine. She and her husband would eat Christmas dinner every year with me and my guy. We would talk about the things we used to do as children. Many times we could get in a place where we were talking and didn't need anybody else because we'd go back to the time when we were so devilish. I felt so bad when that girl left me. She's been dead five or six years now.

Twice a year the circus used to come to town. They had everything there that they had in Coney Island. And they didn't have it where whites could do this and blacks could do that. Inside the tent on Main Street, there was a big old space and everybody sat in there together to see the elephants and the tricks.

If you got on the merry-go-round, you was with your own people. When you was on the Ferris wheel, you was with your friends so you gonna get in the seat and the white one don't have to get in that seat. What I really liked was those merry-go-round swings. The regular merry-go-round was like the little horses and seats but the merry-go-round swings went 'round and 'round, and they swung all the way out there, way out. I didn't get scared when I went up in those things. When you're young, you're crazy.

Little bands used to come into our town and play in a big old club like a dance hall with seats around. They sold candies and cookies in the back. The whites weren't there but some-times the police would come and stand back there and watch us dance. Sometimes a few of the whites would come. They'd get behind the counter and look at us but they would never get out there on the floor.

Years ago when the music was playing, the white people couldn't even tap their feet in time to the music. We'd say they couldn't dance. I don't say that no more. White people can really dance today. They can dance like mad; they can get down. It's a different generation. The white kids can dance just as good as the colored kids now. I think that you are born knowing how to dance. Believe it or not, little babies have rhythm even in the crib. You give a little colored baby a stick and see how he hit it on that crib with a timed beat. You can find a little colored baby in a crib and he'll be tapping on something. Oh, yes, you're born with it; you can hit and make music without anybody playing behind you. It's just the way you're rapping it.

Don't ever ask a colored kid how he learned to dance. A colored person is born dancing. If you find somebody that say he can't dance, there's something wrong upstairs. You know they say that we got rhythm. We were born dancing. We like music. I would say that everybody ain't got it for singing but dancing is something else. I could stand in one place and do as many dances as you could do all over the floor in a dance hall.

We had a place in town that had a piccolo in it. (That was a juke box but in those days we didn't call it a juke box. It was a piccolo.) It was in a pretty-good-sized place, and the part with the piccolo in it was where you danced. We'd say, "A nickel for the piccolo." We'd say, "Put the money in the piccolo and let's dance." There were about three of those places in Denmark. The one I used to go to, we called it the better one.

You'd walk in the door and it was a whole big place with the piccolo sitting over there. Behind the piccolo were tables and chairs. On one side was the counter where they sold cigarettes and candy. Around the other way was the kitchen where they cooked fish and hamburgers and other things. Then there was the side where they sold everything in the grocery line. They sold baloney; they sold rice and grits and everything.

Along in that time, the records we had in the piccolo were *Tuxedo Junction* and *Sunny Side of the Street,* all them kind of records. When Ella Fitzgerald made her first record with Chick Webb, *A-Tisket, A-Tasket,* that was the talk of the town. She was a young girl then. I was a young girl. Everybody was young and how we would dance!

We didn't own the house we lived in. How could you own anything when you weren't making anything? In the 1920s, thirties, and forties, no black people had homes. You were lucky to have a shack. Different people would be landlords. They were all white.

We lived in a one-story house. (There were no two-stories in those days. Even the white people in my hometown didn't have two-stories then.)

One time, there was a hurricane. The storm came, hit our house, skipped the next house, and then hit the house after that. Next was the woods and the storm threw the trees down and broke them up and everything. A storm can knock down a bridge with you plunging down in that water and everything. It can knock it down and push it away. Nature is just something you can't do nothing about; just sit up and pray, that's all. I don't care how many boards you put up, you still have nothing to keep the storm from tearing the house down. There's nothing you can do unless you have something deep in the ground. I'm talking about deeper than just a basement. If you have a deep cellar, that might work. You might escape. 'Cause when the storm is coming, it takes that house and just breaks it apart.

When that storm hit our house, it took the whole roof off

and laid it over there just like somebody put it there. My sister
Lumisha, she was a young girl then, she jumped out the window and thank the good Lord, she didn't continue going that
way. If she had done that, the roof would have fallen right on
her. So we had a house with no roof for a while, and we had to
stay with some people.

In our house, we didn't have a gas stove or an electric stove.
Everything was wood and it went in the stove. Sometimes you
used to have a potbelly heater in the living room. You were a
big shot if you had one of those. And we had a fireplace, too, to
keep warm. We would carry wood from the woods just like a
human wagon. First we would go and cut wood. Then we'd get
two long poles and lay them down. We'd put the wood across
them two poles; we'd stack it up. Then one of us, like me or
my brother or my sister, would get in front and grab up them
two poles and the other would get back there and grab up the
two poles. Sometimes it sure was heavy. Sometimes one of us
would get angry with the other one and drop the poles. Then
we'd have to pick up all that wood and put it back on our
human wagon. But still, God knows, we used to have some fun
in our day.

We didn't have running water or a bath or a sink. We took
a bath in a big old tin tub. Now you didn't have just one tub;
you had to have about five tubs for our family. In the wintertime, we would have to put pots on the stove to heat the water
and then throw it in the tubs. In the summertime, it's so hot
down South, we could heat the water with sunshine. You fill
that tub full of water and sit it out in the sun for an hour and a
half. That tub gets just as hot as hot can be. Sometimes you
would even have to add a little cold water in it. After it got
heated up, you had to bring the tub in the house. The tub had
two handles on it and somebody would help you carry it.
Somebody would take one side and you'd take the other side.
That's how we took our baths.

I don't know how we did it with eight children but we

did it. Nobody was dirty. Everybody was clean. We all had a chance to take our baths. We took them on Saturday in the day because the older boys and the older girls would want to be out on Saturday night.

In my day, there weren't any washing machines. You would have to boil the clothes in a big old iron pot. You had to wash the clothes in a tin tub and scrub them. There was no stuff like bleach or that. We washed clothes and rinsed them and hung them on a line outside. And the sun took care of that too. The sun took care of everything.

We didn't have a bathroom, we had an outhouse. You could look down in the hole that you got to sit over and sometimes you could see a snake in there. I can't stand snakes. Every time I think about a snake, my skin crawls. When I was a kid I never played with them in the yard. I wasn't afraid of them, because I used to kill them. But now I'd give that snake all the right-of-way he wants. I'd walk a mile around him to keep from killing him. I once heard somebody say, "Oh, there aren't any snakes in the South anymore." But one of my girlfriends who moved back down there said, "Freddie Mae, don't let them fool you. There are snakes here all right."

I hated that outhouse so much when I was young. I said that if I ever got grown, I would never use one of those things again, even if I had to buy a bucket or a pail. I'd buy me a slop jar before I used those toilets again.

Things have changed down South: Now they won't let an outhouse be within the town limits. Most people got bathrooms and toilets now. Most of the factories and things like that went south; people started making more money and they got their own homes and trailers. People that didn't have a stick when I left South Carolina, you should see what they got today. Oh, it's really beautiful down there now. Everybody has got their own house. If I had of stayed down there, maybe I might have had me one too, who knows?

Denmark is much bigger now; people have built homes in the fields where they used to plant corn and cotton. You can't go through those fields anymore because you'd be going through people's property now. My town is not a little town anymore.

My mother was only forty-nine years old when she died. She wasn't sick before she died—like you say somebody was sick a long time—unless she was hiding it. She wasn't in bed where you had to take care of her. I don't know the cause of her death. She pained like everybody else pained, you know, like stomachache or headache or backache or whatever. But nobody did say why she passed. She just died suddenly.

Momma died at home. There were no hospitals in my town at that time; the closest one was in Charleston or Columbia. Everybody was in the house but Willie, the oldest, who was living with his wife and family. Henry was there, Maggie, Julius, and myself. Henry could see that she wasn't responding and so he told me and Maggie to go over to Willie's house and tell him to come over there. You had to walk but it wasn't too far. (When you're in the South, a mile is just a little walk; we walked everywhere.) Willie got there real fast.

That was one of the worst days of my life. I was sixteen and I was so scared. She died on the 3rd of January, 1940. I'll never forget that date as long as I live. Every year, I mark that date on the calendar: so-and-so many years since Momma died. And every year that goes by, there's another year. Nobody talks about my mother but me. Now if I bring it up, they'll say some things that they remember about her but nobody don't make the first move.

I just wish my mother could've lived to get older. I thought I would never get over it. Time helps but I still think about her and she's been dead almost sixty years. One day, I'm gonna meet her. You watch what I tell you. I'm gonna meet my mother because I loved her. I don't have a picture of her. In the days back there when my mother was coming along, there wasn't too many people making pictures with cameras. When you're poor, you don't have no camera. So how you gonna make a picture without one? You didn't even know anything about a camera in those days.

I didn't have any picture of myself as a little girl either. I wish I had a picture of me then. I would love that. I would blow it up and make it so big and pretty. The only time you got your picture taken was in school. They always had a class picture. A fella that was in my second-grade class told me he had a picture of me when I was in the first grade. I begged that boy to please let me borrow it and have it made over and I would send it back to him but he never did do it. I don't have any pictures of me as a real young girl, only as a grown girl. The older people who knew my mother say that the older I get, the more I look like my mother. And oh, I feel so proud when they tell me that. It's almost like they hug and kiss me.

When Momma died, Daisy was married, Victoria was married, and Willie was married. Lumisha died five years before my mother. Henry was old enough to be married but he was still in the house. Me and Margaret and Julius weren't married. My mother didn't live to see all her grandchildren. Her first grandchild was Daisy's son. She saw him. She saw only three of Victoria's children. She didn't live to see but one of Margaret's children, the oldest son. And Willie didn't have his little girl yet.

When Momma died, four of us was gone and four was still in the house. We four just stayed in the house together; we had to do the best we could. The older brothers were working in the fields for the farmers; they would bring in a little money. It wasn't much. I went to bed many nights without a meal.

Today, you can come to my house any time you want and always get a meal. Because I promised myself that if I ever got grown, I would always have plenty of food in my house.

SISTERS AND BROTHERS

My sister Victoria is named after my grandmother. Victoria is a beautiful name. Margaret has a beautiful name too. I don't know why they had to name me Freddie Mae. I wasn't named for anybody. It's not Fredericka. It's Freddie. The reason why I got two names, why they put the "Mae" on me, is that they just didn't want to say Freddie for a girl. When someone says Freddie, they're looking for a man but then a woman shows up. That's what used to get on my nerves.

I hated that name, Freddie. I wished they had called me nothing. Looked like I could adjust to it but it's so hard. That's why I made the people back home called me Freddie Mae Baxter. I made them say my whole name. Now my people from home, they know to say Freddie Mae Baxter. If a car passes and someone calls out "Freddie Mae Baxter," I know it's somebody from home. I used to go to these cookouts in Brooklyn where people from home would be sitting around. When they saw me, they'd say, "Freddie Mae Baxter. Freddie Mae Baxter." And it makes me feel like bouncing, like a little baby when he's clapping his hands.

In the South, almost all of us had nicknames. My mother's name was Julia but everybody called her Miss Teedee. Henry was Buck and Willie was Bill. We called Daisy Deedee. We called Margaret Maggie. We used to call Lumisha's husband James, Yearfin. They're just nicknames; I don't know where they came from.

I was hoping that someone in my family would name one of their kids after Momma but not one of them got the name Julia. They don't even have names that we used to have in our day like Rose, Lily, Jesse, Ben. They have names like Keah and them kind of names. I always did say that if I had a child—and if it was a girl—my child would have been named Julia Mae.

Willie had one kid. Daisy had one. Victoria, she had five. Margaret, three. That's all the nieces and nephews that I have. Lumisha didn't have any kids. Henry, Julius, and I had none.

Lumisha died five years before my mother. Daisy is dead. All the other sisters are alive. Of my brothers, Willie and Henry are dead. Julius is alive. Victoria lives in Philadelphia. Margaret is in a nursing home. Four of us dead and four alive. Four of us gone and four left.

Me and Victoria, we don't see each other often but we do talk on the phone. She'll call from Philly and I'll call over there to find out how she's doing. And Julius and I talk twice a day. He'll call me or I'll call him. I wouldn't stay away from my sister and my brother for three or four days without having to know how they're doing. I don't know who's gonna be the last one around here, because one day there's going to be only one of us left. Nobody knows how we gonna end up. I have lots of friends but if I would get ill, I'd want to be with my family.

Lumisha

Lumisha was the quietest sister. She was very short but she wasn't fat. She had long hair and a darker complexion than me. I wouldn't call her beautiful but she was passable. She had a good-looking husband named James. He worked in the field. I loved James to death. I just stayed on him. You hear people talk about how men fumble little girls, how they mess around with them. That man could've done anything to me but he never put his hand nowhere out of place. He always treated me like I was a little doll.

Lumisha was so quiet, she'd say something only if you said something to her. When Lumisha got married, they got their own place, and there was enough space around the house so they could make a garden where everything would grow. Lumisha must have had two green thumbs because everything she touched turned green.

There was a walkway in front of her house and on both sides she had the prettiest flower garden, and all kinds of herbs. She had a vegetable garden in the back. That woman had every kind of vegetable that you could name and they were gorgeous: cabbage, collard greens, turnip greens, mustard, squash, cucumbers, tomatoes, lima beans that she would let run up the fence. (She had her garden fenced in because otherwise people, cows, and goats would come.) And oh, when her sweet potatoes got ripe . . . We were the type of people that didn't have no money to buy nothing so if you got friends and they got a lot of food, they would give you some. Anybody could come and get the green beans that she had. If you came and picked them, you could have them. That's the way we did it.

Lumisha was kind of stingy. She didn't want to give you too much. She'd give you some but it was never enough. Let's say you give me some greens. It should be enough to make a meal. Don't give me just some so that I'm gonna have to put something else with them in order to make a meal. But she didn't do no harm to anybody, thank the good Lord. And I loved her.

Lumisha died young, in her thirties, in 1935. I don't know what she died from because in those days you didn't know. A person just got sick and died. She was sick for quite a spell and we never did find out exactly what was wrong with her. After Lumisha died, we all moved in with James. His house was a big place; it had about five rooms. We called it his house because he worked in the field for the old man who really owned it.

James stayed on for two or three years, then went to another town. He didn't slip off or anything. He told my mother what was happening. But we couldn't stay in that house unless somebody else was gonna go and work in the field. (If nobody was gonna work for the man, we would have to move.) Willie and his wife were already gone. My brother Henry wasn't a field man. So we all had to move into a little house that had two rooms. We all were crowded up in there.

I didn't see James again for a long time. My sister Victoria and her husband were in the same town down South where he went so she got a chance to see him. But we didn't see him because it was quite a distance away.

Willie

Willie was my oldest brother. He was very quiet too. He had a good job working on the railroad. (In those days, you called working on the railroad a good job because railroad jobs didn't ever quit on you.) Willie worked on the tracks, riding on them in a little handcart. They had only one track then for every station; there was no siding and there was no space to put a handcart. And the train would be either coming or going on the same track. So let's say the train was coming around the bend. The men could be someplace where there's a hill. They'd see the train coming and they'd have to take that little handcart and throw it over the hill, then they'd slide down until the train went by. They would have to pull themselves back up and pull that handcart back up there with them. I used to laugh so much when they took that little thing and threw it over and then they had to climb back up after the train go by, but it wasn't funny. It was dangerous. In New York, if they're fixing something on the subway, they got men waving the train down with a lantern. But in those days, you had to figure it out for yourself that a train was coming.

Willie's wife was from our town. We all grew up around each other. I knew her a long time before she and Willie got married. I knew her people. Her grandmother raised her. Willie took good care of his wife. When you worked on the railroad, you could get a little discount pass, and sometimes Willie would get one for his wife to go see her sister in Columbia, 52 miles away. Willie's wife didn't have any children—so she worked to give her something to do. She used to do people's laundry.

Willie's wife tried for a long time to have a baby but she had a couple of miscarriages, and they went for many years before they could conceive a child. The year after my mother died, she had a little girl my mother never got to see, a daughter named Willie Jean. Willie's wife died in 1944, when she was in her early forties. She died in childbirth but they wouldn't tell me about it. But I found out and I went down for the funeral in my all-black funeral clothes. I was twenty-one years old then. Afterward, I went to this little place down South by myself and had a picture made. I wanted a picture of those black clothes.

Henry

Henry was never too steady in his work. He was tall and on the skinny side. He wasn't going to work in the field. He didn't want to mess his hands up. He didn't like dirty work and he wasn't gonna do any heavy work. He didn't want to hurt himself. Henry just wasn't a hard-working man. He could have been a good desk man but he wasn't educated enough to be behind anybody's desk. He would be someplace like on a shanty car, like a caboose, on the railroad, doing the cooking or else helping them take the melons off the trains. You know, that was a few dollars. When you were in the South back in those days, you didn't need to have a whole lot of money. You did what you had to do with what you had.

Henry got married in New York when he was in his forties. He and his wife got along pretty well. First, they were like lovers, then they got married. When Henry came up North, he stayed with me at first and worked on the docks.

The woman Henry married was from Delaware. She was a nurse in a hospital in upstate New York, about the same age as him. They both worked in the daytime so they had plenty of time to be together in the evening. She and Henry didn't have any kids. Why'd you want to have a little baby at that age? If you didn't have it when you were young, you sure shouldn't have it after you get old. They stayed in New York for some years, but when they retired, they decided to move back down to Delaware; she still had relatives there. When Henry went down there, he stopped working and just took up housekeeping. Delaware was where he was when he died, five years after his wife passed on.

Daisy

Daisy was short and not too fat but she was on the chubby side. She married early. Her husband drove a truck for a lumber mill. After the logs got chopped, he put them on this big truck that would take them to the mill. He wasn't getting a fortune but at least it was enough to take care of her and him. Their boy was my mother's first grandchild. Daisy said she didn't want any more kids. I don't know why she wanted only one. (You could say she was better off than me, though. At least she had one.)

Her husband was pretty abusive to her. I knew he was doing her in but I couldn't do anything about it. If you don't want it, you should leave. If somebody's doing you in and you gonna stay with him, the family should leave you alone. The family should never get involved in it because if he goes off, he's gonna hurt the family and you and everybody else. Daisy took it for as long as she could, then she left and came North by herself. She left her husband down there. They just quit.

Daisy and her husband were together a long time before she came up North. They got married in the early thirties and she came up North in the late forties. My brother Bill took care of her son, John. We called him Bubba. Daisy never did go back South. After somebody told her that her husband had passed in the 1950s, she went back just for a visit.

Victoria

Victoria is about six years older than me. She's a little taller than I am and she looks something like me. And she's closest to me, having the same outgoing personality. There's some people that can be in a place for weeks and they don't talk to anybody. But anyplace that Victoria goes, she can always find somebody to start a conversation with. Anyplace she goes, she can make a friend.

Back home, Victoria worked in the field. There was no jobs around, only fieldwork. She got married down home when she was around twenty and her first child was born when she was twenty-one. Her first husband had a good job. He worked in a mill, bringing in the logs and cutting the lumber. Soon as they got married, they moved to another town called Sumter.

Victoria really didn't work after she got married. She had five kids, four girls and one boy. She made her children and that was it. Three of them were born in Sumter; the other two were born in Philadelphia.

Victoria had all five kids with her first husband and none with her second husband. But her first husband just didn't do her right. You don't have to hit somebody to be abusive. You can do it mentally. He didn't give her the respect I thought that she should have. He was a minister, a great talker. I thought one time they would never break up because he was a minister. He went to Philadelphia with her and they broke up there. They're both still in Philadelphia and he's still alive.

Victoria is on her second marriage now. She's been with this guy for forty-two or forty-three years. It's a beautiful marriage. The kids loved Victoria's second husband and they still love him. She should've had that marriage first. Those two people love each other. They have a sense of something that you want to just sit back and listen to them. They don't try to make each other feel out of the way. Some men can say something that can make you feel bad. But those two people are there in each other's corner. I hope she goes before him. I really do. Because if he went first, I don't know if she could handle it.

Her husband worked on the railroad, not as a conductor or anything like that. He was a train cleaner. He would clean in the station and also on the train. He didn't travel. He worked on that railroad for many years until he retired.

Victoria raised all of her kids in Philadelphia. Two of her girls, Carol and Josie, finished school. I think her daughter Carol went to college and Josie went. The other two girls didn't go to college and the boy didn't. After Josie got married, she started having kids so I don't know what kind of work she did. I know her husband had a pretty good job. He was a builder. Josie's son Spencer went to college. He didn't want to do no hard work. He wanted to be behind a desk. And that kid is a smart kid. I think he works in the post office and he likes it. Handling the mail is not too big a thing. He's been working there for quite a few years. Lily Mae, the other daughter, takes care of some kids, and her first son is in college down South.

Victoria is right there in Philly now. You just don't know where you're going to choose to live. You go to that place and probably like it and that's where you stay. Victoria lives in a one-family house. Just she and her husband live there now. The sleeping quarters are upstairs. All of Victoria's children have their own families now, and all her children except for one raised their kids right there in Philly.

One of my nieces has seven kids. Another one has three. Another one has two. And another one also has two. Victoria has grandkids and great-grandkids. They all live about fifteen or twenty minutes from Victoria's house by car. They can see each other Thanksgiving, Christmas, and everything if they want to. I really love the kids. I love my people. I love to grab them and hug them and stand off and look at them. And I say, "When you say that I can't hug you no more then you can forget about it. 'Cause I think that I'm supposed to hug you until I get where I can't hug no more."

I don't see them too much now like I used to. I can't get around like I used to. When I go to Philadelphia now, I don't have no time alone with Victoria because the kids get around me and they want to take me someplace. But I still have fun with my sister. We could spend the time right there in the house, talking about people that we haven't heard from or if we think they're dead or not dead or whatever.

Victoria is a great talker. Sometimes I get on the telephone with her and I wish I had enough money so we could just talk, talk, talk. We get a kick out of each other. Even though Margaret and I are closer in age, I have more to talk about with Victoria. She's always got something going and I always got something going. If she calls me, she'll say, "You gotta send me money for the phone bill." But it's just joking.

Victoria is about eighty years old now. She's not doing too well on her walking but she really was a person that didn't

just flop down. She always was up and going and now that she
can't walk too good, she still got that spirit. When you say,
"How you been?" she'll say, "Oh, I feel fine." She'll never tell
you that she feels bad. I don't have to worry about Victoria
because there's always somebody there to see that she's all
right.

Margaret

Margaret is my difficult sister. She is two years older than
me and she always really knew how to dress. She was a nice-
looking person, not pretty (none of us are pretty), but she
always had lots of fellas around—she really was a very attrac-
tive person. Even if she didn't have but one dress, you had to
look at her.

We were very poor but Margaret would get up and starch
her clothes and iron them. And everything that was a frill
would be standing stiff, not floppy. She could have but one
dress but every time she wore that dress you would think that
she done went to the store and bought a new one.

Margaret is the tallest one of us. She's six something, and
always complained about it. "I'm so tall," she'd say, "I stretch
all the way down here in the bed." I'd say to her, "Nothing you
can do about it. You been tall all your life."

Margaret is difficult, and she was what I would call dangerous because she would hurt you to get what she wanted. If you
fought with her, you would really get hurt. Everybody was
scared of Margaret. She didn't need nobody. She could protect
herself, she could fight like an alley cat.

I didn't fight a lot with Margaret 'cause I didn't want to be
hurt. I hate being hurt mentally and physically. I don't want
you to hurt my heart and I don't want you to mess up my skin.
So Margaret and me didn't do too much fighting. The way you
had to keep from fighting was to let Margaret have her way.

Long as you did that, she'd think you were the greatest. But when you say no to her, you better watch out.

Margaret wanted you to do things her way. But I don't want nobody to have to tell me what to do, where I can't voice my opinion about it. So we'd have a little fight. Margaret and me mouthed a little bit. We would talk some and maybe I would walk away and go about my business. But I would compromise and do some of the things she wanted to do. Whenever something went wrong, I couldn't stay away from my sister for long. I'd have to talk to her and say, "Let's try to get this thing straightened out. If I did something to you, let me apologize." I don't want it to stay like that. I don't want to be mad at my sister. I love her. We'd have a little misunderstanding but we'd get it straightened out that day.

Margaret is not going to apologize to you. She'll say she's wrong but she just don't want to apologize. She just don't want to be the under. (If you say something out of the way, then you go back and say "I'm sorry I said so-and-so," that means you're the under.) Margaret always wants to be the over. I think the opposite. I think if you can't apologize, you're an under. You're a little person, very small. You're supposed to be big enough to apologize if you did wrong. Now, if you're right and you know that you're right, I really don't think it's up to you to apologize. But if you're wrong, I don't think you should say to yourself, "I know I'm wrong but I'm not gonna apologize." Margaret is like that. She just don't want to be the under. And up until today, I think we all let Margaret have her way. We just call her "our sister that we let have her way." And, you know, I think it ruined her as a grown-up.

Margaret liked tall men. She loved them real tall. If you want to get on her nerves, start talking to her about a short man. If you said, "I'm going to introduce you to a short man," she'd say, "Oh, no, you don't. You keep him for yourself." There was one guy from our town who used to work with the circus, the one that came to Denmark twice a year. He traveled with the circus when they went from city to city. He was her first love, a teenage love, but they got away from each other.

Margaret married pretty late. Her husband was a farmer, and they had three kids. There was an older boy and a set of twins, a boy and a girl. Margaret didn't raise her kids. She left her husband when the twins were about five years old, and she came up North by herself. Her husband and his mother raised the kids. So that means the kids didn't know much about Margaret.

We don't know where her older boy is, he just went away. Nobody knows whether he's dead or he's alive. I ask people when they go home to find out about him but nobody can tell them anything. I haven't seen him since he was in the third grade. If he's alive, he's got to be some place around. One day I might pay some money to try to have them look him up. One of the twins died. The girl is alive but the boy is dead. The only one left is the girl; she lives in Brooklyn now.

Julius

Julius and I are still very close. He's my baby brother, five years younger than me. My mother died when he was only about twelve years old. A few weeks after she died, her brother and his wife, who lived in Elizabeth, New Jersey, wrote down home and said they would like to take my mother's youngest child. They never could have children of their own. I wanted that child to be me. Oh, did I want that to be me! But I was more than sixteen. I was too old. People don't want to start with you as a teenager because they figure you're all ready to go and make trouble. They figured they would be better off raising a twelve-year-old boy than a sixteen-year-old girl. I think they did right. Now I'm glad they didn't take me, because maybe I wouldn't have turned out to be who I am. But oh, how I cried when my Julius had to leave me down there.

My uncle took Julius and raised him up from a twelve-year-old boy until he got to be a man. Julius loved his uncle and aunt. He could've left a long time ago if he had wanted to but he stayed with them because he loved them. They never did have children of their own. The wife thought he was her own child, and I think that's why they got along with Julius so good.

When we were little, if I had two cents and my brother Julius wanted one, I would give it to him. Right now when we're old people, we're still close. If he's got something and I want some of it, he gives me some of it. And if I got something and he wants some of it, I give him something. And we don't have to ask each other for anything.

Julius acts like I'm his momma. Anything goes wrong, he makes sure he lets me know about it. Just like you would call your mother and say, "Mom, I hurt in this place." Or "I got to go to the doctor. Would you meet me at the doctor's office?" That kind of way. I always called him Momma's baby.

Julius is more bashful than me, but if you start him up, he'll outtalk a talking machine. Wherever he went, somebody knew my brother. Julius finished high school in Jersey, but when he was about eighteen, he left Jersey and came to New York. He was called to the army during World War II. You can bet your bottom dollar he didn't volunteer. He was over there in France for quite a spell. Once when he was in Paris, I baked him a great big layer cake and sent it over. I'm really good at coconut cake, which Julius loves. That's the kind I sent. He wrote me a letter and said the fellas went crazy over it. I sure wish I had kept that letter. After the war, Julius worked cleaning the subway as a porter. Now he is retired. He's so glad he's retired.

If anything happens to Julius, I swear to God I don't know

what kind of condition I would be in. I'd have to say what the undertaker should do and take care of the funeral. And though I am always the one in the family doing this, if it was Julius, I don't know if I'd be able to do that. I just don't know.

Even more than with Victoria, Julius and I can get on the telephone and we can talk, talk, talk. And he can come to visit me or I could go to visit him and we can just sit up in the house all day long because he likes so many things that I like. I like to play cards, he likes to play cards. I like to go to Atlantic City, he likes to go to Atlantic City. We say, "Next time we go out to Atlantic City, we gonna break them."

And if it gets so his lady don't want to go to Atlantic City or my friend don't want to go, me and Julius go together, just the two of us and we have a good time.

Julius never married. He has a lady, a nice settled lady I've known for over forty years. He brought her to the house like I was his mother. She don't ever forget my birthday. She'll call to say "Happy birthday" or that she's sorry So-and-so died. But she don't call just to talk. I said to Julius, "When you gonna get married?" And he said, "When you get married." I said, "Man, you'll have to wait until you get to be a hundred years old."

He's always saying that it's all over with his lady friend, that it just ain't working. The other day he called and said, "Freddie, I swear it's the end." I said, "Don't swear to me, because I know you. You gonna go right back."

I think he tells me that just to see my reaction. He wants me to say something like, "If I was you, I wouldn't bother with her no more." But instead, I put her way up on a pedestal. I don't know what's happening between them, but I really know that he likes her: if he didn't, he wouldn't keep going back. So I'm always right there on her side. I told Julius, "You have to take her as she is. You can't know a person for all these years and then all of a sudden, she got to change. She's who she is and that's how you got to take her. You take her for what she is and you'll get along."

I think the sister should pretend to like her brother's lady whether she does or not. (Now I don't mean that I dislike his lady, because I do like her.) I think if you want to keep your brother, you should try to get along with his lady. Because she can give him something that you can't give him. And she can take him away from you. He will not come to see you if you don't like his lady. You know a sister-love and a lover-love are two different things. They shouldn't be nowhere near each other, because a brother and a sister got one love here and the brother got another thing there. You shouldn't make that go together. I'll always be his sister but he can divorce his lady friend. He can't divorce me.

Julius tries to get me involved because I'm his listener. Like if he's mad at his lady friend and he comes to me, I don't say anything. I just listen. He wants me to argue with him but I just let him go ahead and knock himself out. So when he's got that pressure off him and he's feeling good, he can go about his business.

When my brother turned sixty-eight, I made him that same coconut layer cake he likes and I had the letters "68" on the cake. I bought him the cutest card you ever laid eyes on, that says "To My Special Brother." On the back of the card is a beautiful automobile, very black and shiny. Now you got to turn the card over and there's a picture of a big old cockroach with a black shiny back and down there it says, "Well, I did the best I could on my budget." That really made him laugh.

All our life Julius and I were like that with each other. Now we both live alone. Every day, twice a day, we're in touch; at night and in the morning. We don't go to bed without calling on the phone and asking, "Are you all right?" And the same thing whenever we wake up in the morning. He don't get up in the morning without ever finding out whether I woken up. And I don't get up unless I find out that he woken up. You can eat something and die overnight. Some people can be in the house for three and four days, and sometimes a week, before you know that they're dead. If I die, he'll know that I died between that hour and to the next morning. Or the next morning into that night. 'Cause we talk every morning and every night to find out whether we woke up or not.

Julius is not in the best of health. He has a heart condition and is overweight but what you gonna do with a man if you're not there to see what he eat? Sometime he'll say he won't eat anything all day because he's thinking it gonna bring his weight down. I say, "That's not gonna bring your weight down." I say, "Eat a little bit for breakfast, a little bit for lunch, and little bigger bit for dinner." The man just don't do the things that I think he should do.

Mostly I think he's feeling sorry for himself. That's what lots of our sickness is anyway, feeling sorry for ourselves. If Julius is down, I play cards with him and curse him out to make him get his mind off himself. If he's got an ace and I got a king, I'll say, "What? You rotten so-and-so. That card should've been mine." And I keep on him like that and he just busts out laughing. I tease him a little bit but nothing to make him feel bad. I like to tell him jokes. When he leaves my house, by the time he gets home, he's feeling all right.

Carol

One of my nieces, Victoria's oldest daughter, Carol, is closer to me than the others. She was my mother's second grandchild. Carol lives in Philadelphia. She almost grew up with me; I'm only thirteen years older than she is. All through my life, she always tried to keep in contact with me. Even growing up as a young girl, she always liked her Aunt Freddie Mae. Not a birthday pass, not a Christmas pass, not an Easter pass, not anything, that I don't get a card from Carol. Sometimes she'll send me a Mother's Day card or a birthday card that might have a little something in there for me. It makes me feel very good. I can lay up in bed and think about Carol and she'll call me and say, "I just wanted to say hi." I love that. You don't have to give me anything. Just love me.

Carol is in her sixties now. She was married to an older man and she had three boys. Her husband died some years ago. The middle boy died but the other two are still alive. Carol is a nurse and she still has to work. She's on the night shift now—from five or six at night till the next morning.

Carol sang professionally for quite a few years. She had her own band. I went several times to hear her sing. The place was filled up with people and everybody was yelling, "Carol! Carol!" She could upset a joint in a minute.

I don't know for sure where she learned that singing, but I think it was in church. Once Margaret's church in New York hired Carol's church choir to come up from Philadelphia and sing. During one song, Carol came down off the stage singing and when she got through with that song, she waved to the people and started going back up the stairs, still singing. I enjoyed that so much, I didn't know what in the world to do. I've never been so proud of a niece in all the days of my life. Believe it when I tell you. She still sings in church but she don't sing out now because of working at night; she just don't have the time.

Vicky

I have a goddaughter named Victoria. I call her Vicky; I've known her for fifty-one years, since she was three months old. Her mother was a beautiful lady. I first saw Vicky when I was in my twenties. I was going to work. I was blocks away from my house, when I saw a lady with this baby on her back. I came in behind and this little baby was just looking, looking, looking at me.

The mother was a stranger. I said to her, "Miss. Good morning." She turned around and said good morning. I said, "How old is your baby?" She said, "Three months." I said, "Oh, she's just staring at me." I said to the baby, "Hello, sweetheart." I fell in love with her. I didn't see her anymore that day. But then another time I met up with the mother and I asked her where she lived. She told me she was living in the same building that I was living in but I had never seen her before.

You know how you can click with some people, you can look and tell immediately whether you like or dislike them? Right then, I told the lady that I would like very much to be that child's godmother. She said okay even though she didn't know me from Adam. Today that child is thinking there ain't nothing like me all through the years.

Vicky is a smart kid. She's a receptionist at a hospital. She lives out on Long Island and works nights in the city. She's been married but she's been separated for nine or ten years. She ain't thinking right now about hooking up again. You know it's all right to go and have some fun but like to say getting married again, she says, "Not right now."

When they split up, the husband got the house and she moved into an apartment, then into a house. When I went out there to see the house, I baked a cake and took it to her. (I didn't want to go there empty-handed.) The neighbors said, "Oh, your ma came around." And everybody had a slice of that cake.

I was Vicky's second mother until her real mother died seven or eight years ago, at age eighty-six. Since her mother died, Vicky has called me Mom, and I call her my daughter.

If you're a godmother, you want to buy something for your godchild, and I did when Vicky was smaller. I don't have to buy for her anymore. The only time I buy for her is for her birthday. I give her a nice card then with something in it. She buys little things for me. Sometimes she'll come with a little bottle of perfume, just something to say, "Momma, I love you." And I really appreciate that very much.

Vicky can pick out the nicest cards. Mother's Day. Christmas. Valentine's Day. And they are expensive cards. Vicky's really good. She sends the most beautifulest cards.

You know how some people just don't know how to pick out a card? Carol and Vicky both know how to pick out a card. Anything they send—Christmas card or whatever—you want to keep. They'll send a card that's singing a tune. You open it and it sings. And I tell you the writing on there is out-of-sight. It's almost like they wrote it themselves. I never want to get rid of just those two cards out of all the other Christmas cards that everybody else sends me.

I keep all of them because you never can tell when somebody might say they want some Christmas cards to decorate something, like a church. So when they ask, I'll have them to give. Because I have a whole drawerful of Christmas cards and birthday cards and Easter cards and all these little kind of cards.

I haven't been out to visit Vicky lately because she's over this way more of the time. She always comes to visit me. She was just around the other day. She was seeing a play nearby, so she called and said, "Mom, I was so close and I don't have to meet this friend until seven-thirty so I thought I would just come around." Sometimes she'll call and sometimes she'll drop by. It really doesn't matter because she knows she's welcome here.

MONEY AND GAMBLING

I always tried to get me some money. Back home, people wouldn't give you anything. They'd say, "Freddie Mae, come here. I want you to go to the store for me." I'd go, come back, and give them the stuff and that was it. They could've said, "Oh, this child did this for me and I'm gonna give something to her to make sure that she know that I'm all right." Sometimes they would say thank you, but I wasn't thinking about no thanks. They should've at least given me a nickel. But none of them did. Most of the time in the South when I was a kid, you did everything for nothing.

But still, somehow I'd get me some money. If I'd go by where my mother would be working and I was nice to the kids in the house, the lady would sometimes give me fifteen cents or ten cents, something like that, over my mother's money. And I'd get some other money doing odd jobs for people. Sometimes I could climb up on a quarter. Even though it was only a little bit of money, it meant so much in those days.

If Saturday night come and you got a quarter, it was almost like you was Rockefeller. There was so much you could get with a quarter. You'd get your ice cream cone for a nickel. I liked walnut—that's what we had down there—walnut and peach. One time they had double dips. Oh, boy! And you could get five candies for a penny according to what kind of

candy it was. You could get Mary Janes with the yellow outside paper and peanut butter in them. And the silver bells that
they call Hershey's Kisses up here. You got five of those for a
penny. But I wasn't a candy lover. Every once in a while I'd buy
a piece of candy, but I liked ice cream best of all.

And I didn't spend everything. I could save my money; I
could save part of it. Most of the time, I'd have some of my
quarter left. After the weekend was over, I'd always have me
maybe twelve, thirteen, or fourteen cents. When I went to
school that Monday morning, I'd still have a little change to
buy me something if I wanted to. The other kids, they would
spend the whole thing. When the weekend was over, they
didn't have anything.

When I was a kid, there were so many people around that
it was hard to hide my money. I would tie it in a corner of a
handkerchief and hold the hanky in my hand like it's just an
old rag, and at school, I would take a pin and pin my money
inside my little skirt. Up to today, I can have money in my
house and I can always find me a place that you're not even
going to think to look there. And it wouldn't be locked up no
place. It would just be around. My mother never had no money
to hide. She probably spent it all because she had to feed all
of us.

When I was a young girl, there was nothing to do, but we
made our own fun. We used to have bingo parties—not in a
church, but in peoples' houses; the parents that lived in our
neighborhood organized them. We paid pennies to play the
game. And they wouldn't pay off with no money. If you would
win, you'd get half a pie or a slice of cake, a bag of peanuts or
something like that. What could you get out of pennies?
Nobody made a profit there.

When I came to New York, I liked to go to Coney Island
but you could never win anything on most of the games. But
there was one game I enjoyed, the one that's like you're going

fishing. You got a line and on the end of that line was a ring. Then you had to try and put that ring over the neck of a bottle they had.

The man that ran the game, he kept talking very fast and very loud, trying to get you nervous. But if you were smart, and you pay that man no mind, you could win. You could put that loop beside the bottle, move it up very slowly—and paying him no mind—you could get it up to the top and twist it over. I won a lot of prizes at that game. I got little dolls and little teddy bears. You know that man ran me away from that game. He said to me very quiet so nobody could hear, "Go away!" I didn't get mad. There was no need for me to start up with him, because the man could see that I wasn't paying him any attention or getting scared of him. I have my own mind. If I'm gonna do something and I'm doing it, you can holler all you want.

What money I made when I was a kid was mine. Same as when I was grown. I didn't have any kids and that meant I was a little better off. So I did very good for my family; I could help my sisters and brothers, and I could buy things for my nephews and nieces. They used to call me the good aunt. You know when you're giving, they call you good.

When I would go to visit my sister Victoria in Philly, all the kids that were in the neighborhood would come to her house to see me. They'd say, "Is that her? Is that the rich one?" Now you know I wasn't really rich, but I would always give the kids something. I was not the type to hold my hand closed.

One year when Victoria's children were small, I bought them a brand-new bicycle with everything on it, everything—the horn, the lights—everything that's supposed to be on a bicycle was on there. They never had a bicycle before. I bought just one bicycle for them all. They had to share it. I didn't say, "It's for you" or "It's for you." I said, "It's for the house." They really think about it even today, now that they are all grown and everything. Every once in a while, they turn around and give me a little something.

When I was working, I knew where my next money was coming from. There are things I used to do then that I wouldn't do now that I'm retired. Every once in a while I used to go dancing, I used to take in some movies.

I used to go to Atlantic City pretty often. Now I don't go all that often—maybe every two or three months. I'm not gonna let my bills get behind since I know I'm not gonna win out there. They say a birdie in the hand is worth a million in the bush. This birdie in your hand is yours. You got it. If you shoot to get them million in the bush, all of them could fly away. So I always take care of business first.

One time I went to Atlantic City for two weeks but I wasn't staying in a hotel, I was staying with people. I didn't go to the casino every day. (If I had money, I wouldn't go there every day 'cause you would get tired of it. Even Rockefeller, when he was alive, didn't go every day.)

For me to go to Atlantic City, I need a piece of money that I can do with what I want to do with it. Not the this-is-for-the-rent money, or this-is-for-the-telephone. I mean money that I can do just what I want with it: buy me something with or go someplace. When I say someplace, I mean Atlantic City. You better not ever let me get hold of a worthwhile piece of money. If I had all the money I needed, I'd go to Atlantic City maybe three times a month. I'd go on the first, the fifteenth, and the last of the month. I'd have me a good time.

I really do love going to Atlantic City. Thank God it really is something that I can enjoy. 'Cause I need some enjoyment in my life. I done worked. I done helped. I had to have some fun because when I was dealing with the people I was working for, I needed something that I could just hang out by myself. Like if you feel bad or whatever it is, gambling will take it away from you. You can have a pain and it makes you forget it.

That's why you see so many crippled people out there. They're on crutches and in wheelchairs and with walkers. Even blind people are there. When you go, it takes all that away from you for a while. Because you're there with your little slot machine and when you're winning a little something, you forget everything. It's true, so help me God.

So many people go to the casinos, sometimes you'd be in Atlantic City and you'd swear that ain't nobody else left in New York. And they come from different directions, too— from South Carolina, from as far as Washington, D.C., and Connecticut. They come there from all over the world. There's money out there. Jersey's cleaning up, man. I wish they'd put casinos in New York. Then us New York people could make some money.

The bus that we go on stops at two casinos: Bally Park and Trump World. I like to go to Bally Park. That's where I won my first money. I think that was the first time I ever won any money. I can go to the Taj Mahal after I go to Bally because you can walk up on the boardwalk to the Taj Mahal if you want to. (You should see that place. Outside and inside, it's gorgeous.)

Old Mr. Trump, he's got four places in Atlantic City. He's got four of them suckers out there now. He's got Trump Plaza, Trump World, Trump Castle, the Taj Mahal. And those casinos are all filled up.

All the casinos in Atlantic City are so pretty—all the chandeliers and the beautiful floors and mirrors—so pretty, it looks like you wouldn't want to gamble. They make them beautiful to get people's eyes. They want to make theirs prettier than the others. I don't go there for the beauty. I couldn't care less about beauty. I could sit right on the floor and play.

When you go to Atlantic City on the bus, you pay for a round trip. It's about a three-hour ride. It's a long day, especially when you get broke early.

When the bus lets you off, you go right in the casino. The

lady comes and tells you, "Welcome to So-and-so casino." She says, "Have your bus ticket stub out." Then they give you another ticket and you go to the change booth and get a rebate—money to play with, which they give you as a ten-dollar roll of coins, a five-dollar roll of coins, and two dollars just in quarters. Then if you gonna get some more money to gamble with, you can get it while you're there, where you won't have to come right back.

I once got left behind by the bus but it wasn't my fault. I was with Julius and Margaret, who was on her first trip to Atlantic City. Everybody is told when the bus is getting ready to leave but I guess she just forgot. Anyway, when the time came for the bus to go back, my brother and I were on there. Everybody was on that bus but my sister Margaret.

If they tell you to be there and you're not there, they gonna leave without you. That afternoon, I looked all around for Margaret. I didn't see her anywhere. The man tried to wait. But I knew I couldn't leave her behind. So I told him to go ahead on. So then Julius said he wasn't going to leave me out there by myself, looking for Margaret. So the bus went off and left us.

We found her in the casino. Maybe she was winning a little something. You're just playing and if you're winning, you done forgot whether you came on the bus or whether you came by airplane. Julius was so mad. He grabbed Margaret and said, "Why weren't you there when they said, 'Let's go'?"

I said, "There ain't no reason to get mad." I said, "What is money? Money is something you can't do but two things with: Spend it or save it." That's the only two things to do with money. Now you could give it away but that's just as if you're spending it. So we just went over to the Greyhound line and we bought some tickets. We spent extra money for the bus but what are you gonna do? The Greyhound bus brought us to Forty-second Street; then we caught a subway and went uptown. And you know we got home before the other people did.

I sometimes go to Atlantic City with Vicky, the girl I call

my daughter. She'll go with me anytime I ask her. But not one quarter will she gamble because she doesn't want to spend her money that way. And she doesn't try to make no bones of it.

There's lots of people that don't gamble. But the majority do and I'm one of them. Vicky goes on the boardwalk; she goes on the beach; she goes shopping. The last time we went together, she bought some little jars of spices for the kitchen and a big old bag of peanuts.

When I go to Atlantic City, I don't even go to the bathroom because I feel that it might be my lucky time in the casino, the time I'd hit the jackpot. I don't think about eating in the casinos either. I eat before I get off the bus and I eat again when I get back on. Some people may say to me, "Let's go get a sandwich." But you won't ever get a sandwich with me in the casino. When I go in there, something grabs me: I want to go right on, looking for a machine to start playing.

I have played blackjack but I have never played dice. That's for big rollers. There's a game called backarack. It's something that the big people play. You got to have big bucks to be in there. I wouldn't even look in it. I never asked anybody how it worked.

With the slot machines, you can hang out by yourself. You don't need no friends. I don't care who I'm with. I get blind because there's so many machines in the casino and you don't know which one to play. So you just play and if you're lucky, you win. If you're not lucky, you won't win. That's all. I realize you can lose but that's not the point. The point is that in your mind, it's gonna be your day. And one day, it's gonna be your day.

When you play the slot machines, you can either pull the handle or they have buttons. I prefer using my fingers on the buttons. Years ago, before they had buttons, my arm would get sore because it looked to me like I wanted to hurry up and win the money. You want it to come so bad. You just go so fast.

They also have these machines that you can put your twenty-dollar bill in there or your ten-dollar bill and your change will drop in the pan. But I don't want to do that 'cause every time I put the bill in there, it shoots back out. And I think that one of these days that machine is gonna tear the sucker up. And they have little machines in the casinos where you can put your credit card and get money from them. All you have to do is put your card in and you get your money when you want it. Some people use those cards but I don't ever do that. I know that when I come back home, I'll owe somebody a hundred dollars or fifty dollars or whatever. (What I lose out there, I want it to stay out there.) And I would never use one of them cash machines that they have in the bank either. I'd rather go in there and go up to that window and let those people give me that money. Then I'd stand someplace and count it out.

You know they have quite a few clubs in Atlantic City. They have different big stars in there. Sometimes they have a band right there on the floor in the casinos. If you want to dance, to shake it a little bit, you can. But all I wanted to shake was pulling the handle on that slot machine.

I tell you something happens to you out there in Atlantic City. Your mind is addled. Your mind is so much on wanting to win them people's money, you could forget yourself. If you're not on the ball, you can forget about time and everything because outside the casino is life and in there you just got *your* life.

It's like an amusement park. They just want you to have fun. When I lose, I don't get angry. What about the time when I win? That's why you should be a good sport. If you win some time, you aren't mad at nobody. So if you lose some time, you shouldn't be mad at anybody. 'Cause they don't wring your arm to come.

They say it's beautiful there but it can get ugly. That's a lonely place with all that money if you ain't got nothing in your pocket. I don't care if them chandeliers or all them gorgeous things is hanging there. It's not beautiful if I'm broke. There are a lot of sad faces out there, believe it when I tell you. 'Cause you're not going to beat the house, you know that.

When I go to Atlantic City, I decide how much money I'm going to spend and I make sure that I have me about another hundred dollars or so hanging on the side. I take it with me in case I get into trouble. Now that extra money don't get spent. That's in case I get sick or have to go to the hospital—well, you can get in trouble in Atlantic City. You can hit a jackpot and get so happy that you faint. I've seen quite a few people who just can't handle it. I think I'd do all right: If I hit the jackpot, then I'd just hit the jackpot.

My brother Julius, he will spend money in Atlantic City just like that. I tell Julius, "I'm a little person. I just can't afford to spend money like that." I'm kind of chicken about money. So you just remember one thing: If you're lucky, you can win. If you're not lucky, you can't win. Oh, and one other thing—just go to have fun.

If I get broke in Atlantic City, nobody would know it because I don't lend and I don't borrow. You know, you find people who can't say they're your friend unless they want to borrow something. But I want you to be my friend without my having to lend you something. Lending and borrowing: That's not good policy; it breaks up friendships.

When I get to where I have to borrow, you can say something happened to Freddie Mae. I just can't do it. I believe I'd almost be in the poorhouse before I would ask. It just bothers me. Other people are not responsible for you. When you're working, you should try to save a penny here and a penny there and a penny everywhere.

It's such a different atmosphere in Atlantic City than it is in New York City, with the sun and breeze coming off the water. But I don't stay outside when I go there. I go there to gamble. And if you go and win, it's so beautiful.

I went to Atlantic City on my birthday but my money went so fast because I was trying to show off for my birthday. And I got broke real fast. I went on the boardwalk but I didn't want no fresh air. I said, "Okay. If that's the way you want it, I'll catch you next time." Winning is a thing you can't count on.

Every once in a while, maybe every two months, I say, "I think I'm going to play me one of them Lotto cards." One of these days, something will come to me and tell me, "This is your day." And that's when I play Lotto.

The last time I heard about it, the prize was $5 million; sometimes it's $25 million. So once in a blue moon when it says $25 million, I play because I figure that if I don't get them millions maybe I might be in a bracket where only ten people might have it and I'd get a few thousand dollars. I'm not going to think about getting the whole thing. I don't want to have all the millions. I'm not trying to be rich. I'm not greedy. Just give me enough to work with.

Money don't bother me. I never had that much to bother me. But if I hit a million dollars in Lotto, I'm gonna put a lump sum in the bank and say, "You stay there." Not all of it— I would put in maybe twenty-five or thirty thousand. I'd break up the rest and give it to my relatives. My family needs to get their share. I wouldn't keep the money all that long anyway. If I ever get hold of any money, I'm gonna hand it around. I'm gonna give everybody a little taste rather than let Uncle Sam take it. (He going to take his share anyway before I give anybody anything. I realize that.) There'd be so many things that I would like to do, lots of people I would like to help. I used to hand people a lot, you know, but now I ain't got nothing to hand out like I used to. I say, "All I got to give you is that I'll be there if you need me."

·   ·   ·

Money is a funny thing. I really don't want to win millions, it might take my personality away from me. People will do lots of talking when there's no money but when they get their money, it really messes with their mind. I know people who came into lots of money because they won the lottery and they ain't nice like they used to be. They don't care how they treat you or how they talk to you. If I got hold of some money, I would still be Freddie Mae. I would ask God to please don't let me change. Because God knows there's so many people seem to care about me in the way they act. And I wouldn't want that to go by.

If I win a million dollars in Lotto—and that's not even the big prize—then I ain't got no reason to go to Atlantic City. If I got the money already, what the hell am I going for? Going to make more money? No, I'd do something else instead.

But don't worry: I ain't gonna get the million because I don't play Lotto often enough.

I was seventeen when I first came up North. I went to Elizabeth, New Jersey. Most of the kids from the South didn't stop in Jersey like I did. They went straight to New York. I stopped in Jersey because my aunt and uncle, who were raising Julius, lived there.

I got on the train and came on up. (In my younger days, I never was frightened about anything. I would try something and even if it didn't work out, I'd say, "Well, it didn't work out this time. Maybe next time . . .")

When I got to the station, nobody was there to meet me because they didn't know exactly when I was coming. I caught a cab and went 'round to my auntie's house. There were two buildings there, back and front with a yard in between. I didn't know if she lived in the back or the front.

It was in March. It was very cold and I had on a really light coat. By then it was about nine o'clock at night. I was on the stoop of the front building and I hit on the door. Then after a while, I kicked it. I kicked it, but nobody came. Nobody was home.

I heard some children yelling out in the street so I went out and said to them, "My name is Freddie Mae Baxter." One of the little boys said, "Baxter?" He said, "Julius?" I said, "Yeah, Julius is my brother and I don't know where he lives." The boy said, "Come on. I'll take you." And he took me back around in there to the house.

My uncle was still at work but my auntie was at home. I went up the stairs and introduced myself. When I got up there, I was so glad to see my brother. I didn't know what in the world to do. I hadn't seen Julius for about a year. He'd grown some but he was always a little shorty. We hugged and we kissed. We hugged and we kissed.

I wanted to see if I could find a job right away in New Jersey. I went out myself. (My auntie didn't get me a job.) I looked in the phone book for an employment agency and I went there. They called around and found me a little job cooking for a family. I wasn't sleeping-in on that job because I was staying with my auntie.

The day I started working, the lady I cooked for said, "We're going to have leg of lamb for dinner." Well, in the South, you eat your big dinner in the middle of the day at twelve o'clock, then you have a sandwich at night. So I cooked the leg of lamb and got it all ready for twelve o'clock.

When the lady called to find out how I was doing, I said, "When are you coming home for dinner?" She said, "Dinner?" I said, "Yes, the leg of lamb is done." Well, the lady didn't get angry. I got to give her credit for that. She said, "Freddie Mae, we don't eat until about six o'clock. But I tell you what you do. You say the leg of lamb is done. Take it out of the oven. Wrap it up in aluminum foil and just let it sit on the stove. Then when we're ready for dinner, we'll put it back in the oven and let it heat up." And she told me, "Don't fix the other stuff: the vegetables, the rice or potatoes or whatever. Start that about five o'clock." When the lady got home, she talked to me about it. She said, "You're not down South where you eat the big meal in the middle of the day." And she wasn't angry at all.

At that time up North in the forties, if you made twelve dollars a week for domestic work, that was good money. But my auntie told me I had to give her half of what I got. I was still doing chores for her, like scrubbing the floors, washing the windows in her house, sweeping the yard. There was a yard there that two families had to take care of and when it was my aunt's time to do it, me and Julius would do it. I had to do everything that Julius had to do.

I didn't think my aunt should have half of the money I was getting but she was the boss. My uncle just went along with her. I was so upset and unhappy about it. I didn't want to continue giving her half my money. The lady I was working for could see that something was wrong with me, and I took her in my confidence. I couldn't help it. She said, "Why don't you sleep-in here? Take the third floor. You won't have to give anybody any of your money, and you won't have to pay no rent. You won't have to pay for no food."

I could've stayed because the lady asked me to, but I didn't want to hurt my auntie's feelings. So I told the lady no. I didn't want to leave my auntie and go sleep-in someplace. I'd rather go back home down South and if I came back, then I'd be on my own and nobody could tell me what to do and what not to do. So I told the lady no and I told my auntie and my uncle that I was going back home. I came up to Elizabeth, New Jersey, in March and I went back home in July.

When I went back, I had a little money. (I was always the type of person that would save. If I was making fifty cents, I'd try to save fifteen cents of it.) You didn't have to have too much money down there because there wasn't much to do. I was staying with my sister Margaret and her family and didn't have to pay any rent. I had clothes. I could buy a little food. And I started working again.

I was working for one of the richest people in town. They had a clothing store where they sold very expensive things. When you bought something there, you were "Miss Thing."

But I didn't stay with them long. I missed being over there in Jersey. So a few months later I wrote the lady I had worked

for and asked her would she send some money for me to come
back with her. I said that if she would send for me, I would
work for her until I die. And I told her I would definitely
sleep-in. I think that's why she took me back. She had two children. Her oldest daughter was about two or three years younger
than me and her younger daughter was much younger. So
that woman hurried up and sent me a ticket for the train. (In
those days, you could ride the train real cheap. Today it's hundreds of dollars to go back home.)

When the letter from New Jersey came, I had my own
address but at that time there weren't too many street numbers
and different things like that. So the letter went to the post
office. The lady I was working for must've said that if any mail
came to the post office for me, they should bring it to her house
because that's where I worked.

When I got in to work that day, the lady handed me the
letter and said, "Here's your ticket." I don't know if she opened
the letter or not. I felt like an ass. When I first came back
home, I told her, "You know, I'm planning on going back up
North." But I wasn't planning on it. I just didn't know if I was
going back or not. But I knew definitely that I wasn't going to
come back and get a job and then have to give up half of my
salary. If the lady in Jersey hadn't sent for me, I probably
would've stayed on down there.

When I did get back to Jersey, I wanted to see Julius but I
decided I wouldn't go to see my aunt and uncle right away. I
wanted to have me a little stash someplace first. I didn't want
just to come and see them with no money when I couldn't get
my brother anything. They didn't even know I was back in
Jersey. So I just waited until I got myself a good little piece of
money. I must've worked about three months before I saw
them.

The day I went to my auntie's house, you could see her face
light up. She thought that I just got in, and that I was coming
back to stay with her. She said, "Ohhhh. Where's your suit-

case?" I said, "I've been up here now for a good little while. (I didn't tell her how long. I don't like hurting people, you know.) She said, "Oh, yeah? Where you at?" After that I would come to see my brother and give him a little change.

The people that I worked for in Elizabeth, they owned this big clothing store just like the people I worked for down South. When I went back, the lady I worked for didn't pay me twelve dollars a week anymore. She paid me fifteen. I did pretty well there because I didn't have to pay rent. I didn't have to buy food. You ate all the food you wanted. They could buy a whole big piece of meat and everything. And they ate off it only one time. They didn't like to chop it up and use it for leftovers the next day. Whatever they didn't eat was mine if I wanted it. I used to eat so much that sometimes I thought it was coming out of my ears. Those people were really rich and they were very nice to me.

Rita

I wanted company so after about a year or so of working in Elizabeth, I sent for a friend of mine named Rita from back home. I got a job for her, working for the lady's sister. Me and Rita, we used to go all over the place together. There weren't too many places in Elizabeth then for young people to go dancing. But we could go to people's houses and visit.

If our ladies weren't going anywhere that night and their husbands weren't taking them out someplace, they would let us go out, as long as we were back there early enough to get their husband off to his job in the morning, early enough to fix his breakfast. We could say, "Are you all going out tonight?" And if they would say no, maybe I would go to Rita's house and we would be in her room dancing around and playing. If the people stayed home, me and Rita could go out that night even if it wasn't our day off. But when they went out, we couldn't go anywhere because we had to be there with the kids. When I started, I got every other Sunday off, I think it was, and a half-day on Thursdays. That's what it was when you were sleeping-in.

I got a job for my older sister Daisy with another lady in Elizabeth. Rita and I would want to go places around the boys and we didn't want Daisy to come. Daisy had a sleeping-in job when I brought her up North, and her lady didn't want her to go out even if the lady wasn't going anyplace. She wanted Daisy to stay there.

I worked for the lady in Elizabeth for about a year and a half. I used to come to New York on my days off. I'd meet the girls and boys from my hometown there. I knew so many people in New York. You could meet your friends if you went to a place called the Savoy Ballroom. It was a dance hall where I used to meet all of the boys on my days off.

I wanted to live in New York but I didn't say anything to the lady at that time. Then I told her, "I really like working for you but I don't have enough time off for a young girl." The lady was so kind; she started giving me all day Thursday off too. She tried to understand but later on I still had to leave the job. I was young and sleeping-in was bad for young people. There was nothing for you to do. I wanted to get out and enjoy myself. So one day when I had turned nineteen, I told the lady that I wanted to live in New York. Oh, she was so hurt and I hated it so much, God knows I did. I think she offered me eighteen dollars a week but I was just ready to go.

Rita wouldn't come with me. She said she just didn't like New York. I don't know why. And she never did leave New Jersey. She left her job in Elizabeth and got married, moved to Newark, and had three kids. That's where she was when she died a year ago. I feel sad about it. But I think of the good times we had. You know, you think of the good times not the sad times that you had.

New York is a big place but mostly everybody from home

came to Harlem. Some of them went to Brooklyn. The way you'd find out where they were was that someone knows where one is at and tells another and the next thing you know, you're finding out where everybody is at. In the forties and the early fifties, you could meet each other at somebody's house. But the Savoy Ballroom was where everybody wanted to go. It was a big old place. They had two bands there. It cost about a dollar and half to go in, and once you paid your money, you could stay until it closed if you wanted to. You could dance until the wee hours in the morning. I just used to go and dance, dance, dance. The main guy was Erskine Hawkins. His band would be there a whole week, then they'd go and somebody else would come. I got tired of him because he was there too often. I said, "Bring somebody new." But I still danced because I like dancing. It really doesn't matter what music I dance to. Any music you play I will dance to but opera. I might dance to that if I understood it. But I just don't understand it. Any other music, cowboy music, any music you play, I'll dance by it. But my favorite kind is jazz.

New York is my home now. I been here much longer than when I was down South. You know time goes very slow in the South. Down South, it takes a long time for a year to go by. I guess it's because there were not so many things that you could do. There was nothing to do down there but go to school and come home. Then maybe on Saturday you'd go to town, buy you a little powder for your face, candy, or whatever. You'd have a little change and buy a little something, maybe panties or a pair of socks. And it took a long time for Christmas to come down South. In New York, the time goes real fast. A year just goes like you're spinning a top. You can do something for Christmas and before you turn around, Christmas is back.

New York is so great, it have two names: New York, New York. I tell everybody that. They even gave it a third name: Big Apple, New York, New York. This is one of the greatest places in the world. I don't care where you go. Everybody's here. You can't name me a nationality that's not in New York.

In Philadelphia, where my sister Victoria lives, everything is slow. It's not like New York. It's too hard to get around if you don't have a car and you can't drive. Most everybody has a car but I would hate to ask somebody to take me here or take me there. In New York, you don't have to go far for a bus or a train.

When I first came to New York in the early forties, the tallest building in Harlem was the Theresa Hotel. I think it's only twelve or ten floors but that was the tallest building then. Now there's all the projects, all the state buildings, all the banks that were built since I was here. The Theresa Hotel looks like a little bitty thing now.

When I moved to Harlem, it was jivey, it was good. Harlem was so beautiful. Everybody was so good with each other. There was none of all of this fighting and shooting and stuff like that. You could walk in the street anytime of night you wanted and nobody bothered you. Nobody. They might say hello or something like that. But they didn't bother you that you had to be scared to come out of your house. Sure, people would drink. People always drink regardless of what happens but people weren't as bad when they were drinking as they are today. People would drink and fall out in the street and nobody would come and rob them and beat them up. They'd try to help you if possible.

Today, if you fall out in the street, you might think they're picking you up but they'll be robbing you at the same time. It wasn't like that when I first came. It's different people now. What they're doing now are not like the forties people. People don't even know anything about the forties now because they weren't born. Food was very cheap then. I can remember when you could get a loaf of bread for a nickel. Then when it went up to ten cents, everybody started squawking.

About eight years ago, I went down South to a family

reunion. I really enjoyed it. I was only there for a couple of days. None of my immediate family is down there now. No sisters and brothers, nieces and nephews, only cousins. I really would like to go there again just for a visit, say for about a week or maybe two weeks.

But I wouldn't live in the South anymore. For one thing, I'm scared of bugs. When I was living down there, I wasn't scared but now I just can't stand them. All kinds of bugs are running around there. They even got flying spiders.

Like when I was down there for the reunion, I was staying in a motel, and my cousin's husband said, "Now look here, Freddie Mae, I ain't coming down here to kill no bugs for you." But you know when I saw a bug and I hollered "Oh my God," he killed it.

If I was young, I still wouldn't go down South. Even if I get hold of some money, I'm still not going to move back there. I might come and give you a week or two weeks, something like that, but you'll never get me to make it my home again. I just don't like it down that way anymore. When I was down there, I was down there. When I left there, I left for good. I don't think I could handle living down there. It's too dark. There's streetlights when you're in town but they don't go but so far out. Those lights done stop on the outskirts of town, even if it's not quite in the country. If it's really dark, the only lights you see is your automobile lights. I just can't stand it. In New York, the lights never go off. I don't care what time of morning or what time of night it is, you gonna see light.

I was the first of my family to come to New York. All of them eventually joined me, one at a time until nobody was left in Denmark. I brought all of my family up here. The first stop would be my house. They stayed with me. The first one that came was Daisy. The next was Margaret—Margaret or Henry. Then Willie, he came. All of them lived with me when they came up North. Daisy's son, John, he lived with me. All my brothers and sisters came this way, all but Victoria who went to Philadelphia, and Julius in New Jersey.

I would try to get my brothers and sisters jobs. The way my sisters got jobs was that I asked my people where I was working about people that needed somebody. I waited until they worked a few months to give them a chance to get a little bit of money to get straightened out where they could get out on their own. Then I'd tell them they had to move out of my place. They didn't want to leave me but they all did.

Everybody worked out all right. In the 1940s you could walk down one block in Harlem and in every one of those houses in that block—private homes, apartment buildings, whatever—there were signs that said ROOM FOR RENT or KITCHENETTE FOR RENT. All the way down the block.

There's always going to be a leader in the family. They gonna depend on one. In my family, it looked like they all take me as the leader. I'm not the oldest one, you know, I'm almost the youngest but I'm almost the head of the family. And they all seemed like they would depend on me. In New York, I think they depend on me because I got them all here. Anything that happened, it would happen at my house. They would all gang to my house for advice, ask my opinion of different things. And I'd tell them some things like I'm almost head of the family. If it didn't work out, there was nothing I could do about it. Right now if something comes up, I take care of it. Like if somebody dies, I'm the one that sees the undertaker.

If there's a family get-together, I would always be the one to get the family to come to my house for a big dinner or a party. If I'd say, "I'm giving a family get-together and I want you to come," they all would come. Nobody else in the family ever made it up themselves to do it but they all would come to my house.

Families used to get together more. Now everyone's got

their own direction. You got your children and your grand-kids. You might want to have dinner home but everybody is not in the same house anymore. I remember one time when I was working, I used to be serving dinners like nobody's business because everybody would be coming to one house, Christ-mas or Thanksgiving. But then they'd get them spread out and they didn't do it. And it happened with the colored people too. They're not together like they used to be. Here's how it hap-pened. Let's say you have two or three children and you used to go to your mother and your father's house for Christmas din-ner. But when you got a family already, you don't need to leave home to go to somebody's house. Look at how many they would have to feed.

When Daisy came to New York, she did domestic work first. Then, when she decided she didn't want to do that any-more, she went into the hotel business. She worked in a hotel on Forty-third Street as a maid until she retired.

Daisy was nearly seven years older than me but I sort of took care of her. We lived together for about two years and it just didn't work out. I figure when two people are living together, you're supposed to do your part and I'm supposed to do my part. Like I would go out and buy food because I loved to eat. And Daisy loved to eat but she didn't want to help. Just like in that book I remember from the first grade, about the little red hen. When Daisy wouldn't help, I knew she had to go. She didn't want to move out of my apartment; she didn't want to leave me. I don't know if she was scared to go out on her own. So I pet her along. I said, "It would be nice if you had your own place. Then you could go when you want and you could come when you want." And Daisy finally got out on her own. We left friends. I don't want my family out there not speaking.

After that I used to hang out with her a lot. We always had something to do, and we went everywhere together. So much so that the other part of the family used to say, "Well if Freddie ain't coming, Daisy is not coming either."

When Daisy left her husband down South, my brother Willie was taking care of Daisy's son, John—we called him Bubba—until Willie's wife died. Then I went down and brought Bubba back to New York with me. He lived with me for quite a spell from when he was ten until he was fifteen. He was my nephew but he was like my littlest brother. He didn't stay with his mother but Daisy didn't mind that. She had a room that was not far away.

I put Bubba in school and I supported him. I had to. He didn't get much money from his mother. When he came North, he was in the third grade but he couldn't go right on to the fourth grade; he had to go back to the third. (They always put you back when you're from the South. Many, many children that came from the South lost a year.) Bubba was always very slow, though. You had to go over things with him several times before he would get the meaning of it.

I let Bubba go with me when I shopped but I did my own shopping. I don't let nobody shop for me. Whatever you send them for, they gonna bring what you didn't send them for. You send them for butter, they bring margarine. You send them for margarine, they bring butter. When I go, I get what I want and I don't have to go back to the store.

When Bubba stayed with me, I was out working during the day. In the afternoon, he would come home and eat and do his homework. Back then, you could trust the kids to come home when they left school. If they had the key, they could come home. There wasn't any TV or nothing to be watching then. You listened to the radio or played cards. Bubba didn't have to be alone too long because I would be home pretty early. We didn't have no problems. There were neighbors around. Everybody looked out for everybody.

I think you can make it if you have to make it. You can manage if you have to. Only when you don't have to do it, is when you can't manage. That's why when people talk about how they can't go to work because they have children, I say, "There's a way to do it if you really want to."

My apartment was small. Bubba slept on the couch. I made sure that every day he folded up his sheets and put them and the pillows in the closet. In the daytime, you could come and sit on the couch. Then Bubba would make the bed up again at night. In a small place like mine, you make privacy just like the Chinese do. You make a clothesline going across the room with a sheet on it.

When Bubba was fifteen, I told Daisy she was going to have to take him. He was getting big and I was a young girl. (I was only ten years older than him.) I wanted to play. And I didn't want him to get in no trouble. I didn't want anybody to bother me like that—like you hear on the talk shows how the father or somebody in the family did something. Any part of my family that would try to use me like that, I would kill them. I really would. My family is not my lover. So Daisy took Bubba and he lived with her until he got old enough to go out on his own. He left Daisy when he got to be eighteen.

Bubba dropped out of high school. I talked to him a couple of times to see if he would go back but he wouldn't. He done got a little taste of the outside, got going with a girl, and he didn't want to go back.

The first job he got was working in a hospital, a cleaning job. He must've liked it; he stayed there a long, long time. That's where he met his lady friend; she was a nurse. Bubba stayed with that lady for twenty years. He wasn't exactly married but if you stay with somebody for a certain length of time, I call that your wife.

Bubba sang with a little group in his church out in Brooklyn, and he helped the church out with different things. Bubba really did love people. He was a nice friendly guy, easy to get along with.

Bubba died young, in his late thirties. He was very sick. When he died, the preacher was out of town, someplace down past Washington. They must've called him and told him that Bubba had died. The preacher called me and wanted to know whether we would wait for him to come back and do the service. I told him no. I said, "We got this thing together and it will cost more money if we gotta wait for you to come and tell the undertaker to hold it and we don't have that kind of money." I said to him, "If you can't make it back, can't you get the next man down from you to do it, because I can't hold it." And so the preacher came. When I have to talk, I talk. And you got to hear me too.

When Bubba died, they had the funeral in his church, and it was packed. All of us who could come were there. My sister Victoria, four of her children, and her husband came from Philadelphia. The boys in Bubba's group sang, and they left an open space there where Bubba would've been if he had been alive. The boys sang and it sounded just beautiful. And to know that the open space there was Bubba's space. The minister was very good; he really did preach that funeral because he loved Bubba. The people in church spoke so well of him. And that really makes you feel good.

A few years later, Daisy died—of a heart condition, I think it was, but I'm not sure. When her chest would hurt, she always did say she had heartburn. When Daisy walked a couple of blocks, she would say, "I got the heartburn." She would always say that when we were getting ready to go to the bus to Atlantic City or when we was coming back from Atlantic City and we had to walk a few blocks from the bus. Margaret would say, "Oh, let's go on ahead." But I would always stay there with Daisy until she said, "Okay, I'm all right now." Then we would go where we were going. I would stop because she's my sister and I loved her and we were taught to do things for each other. I would do the same for Margaret even though she gets mean.

When Daisy died, it caught me off-guard. She took sick one morning. It was about ten and her girlfriend happened to come by. Daisy yelled out the window to her and the girlfriend asked what was wrong. Daisy threw her keys out the window and told the girl to come up. The girl said she didn't even know what key would open the door but the first key she put her hand on, that's the one that opened the door. She went up there and Daisy looked so bad, the girl called 911 right away. When they came, they put something over Daisy's nose. Then they took her to the hospital and she died.

Daisy's girlfriends came over and tried to find me but I was at work downtown. They found my friend Bernice who wasn't working that day and they told her. What Bernice should've done was call me at work and ask me to please ask my boss could I come because something happened. But Bernice just told me then and there on the phone that Daisy had died. I started to scream and scared the lady I worked for half to death. If I had been home and they called me and told me that she died, I wouldn't have gone on like that.

Daisy was a diabetic. I think she killed herself, not meaning to. I believe that she went to the drugstore that morning and bought some cough syrup. When I went to Daisy's place later, I could see cough syrup spilled all over the place. The medicine that she usually took—her insulin and everything that she had to take with needles—maybe that medicine wasn't supposed to go with that syrup. Maybe that started her heart beating too fast. If you are a diabetic, any kind of medicine you take—heart medicine or whatever—you can't just take any of that medicine over the counter. I bet you any amount of money Daisy wasn't supposed to take that cough medicine with insulin and whatever medicine she was taking.

· · ·

My older brother Willie came to New York in 1947 with a child and no wife. (His wife had died.) He waited until his little girl, Willie Jean, was about three years old. When he came up with the little girl, he stayed with me. Willie got work on the docks. He used to work nights so we made arrangements to take care of his child: I would be with her at night, he would be with her during the day. Willie remarried here in New York. His wife was from home but she came up here and they got married here. He didn't have any more children, just that little girl. I liked Willie's second wife very much because she was good to that child. Willie Jean was five or six when he remarried.

The little girl went to school in New York but when she was ten years old, Willie wanted her to go back down South to go to school and I took her back there myself. She stayed with her grandmother, that is the mother of her stepmother. Willie Jean liked it down South with all her friends. She stayed down there until she was about fourteen, then she came back up this way and finished up in school here. Now she's a grandmother herself with four grandkids. I tell you, they can be little like that and the next thing you know, they're president of the United States.

When my difficult sister, Margaret, came to New York, she stayed with me awhile. After she got straightened out, she left. Margaret and the guy from the circus down South met back up again here in New York in later years. They got married and stayed together for a long time. He was Margaret's second husband. He had a good job; he was a dry cleaner in a tailor's place downtown in a nice neighborhood. Big people used to bring him their clothes. They didn't want anybody else to take care of them but him. Like the movie stars will have a spot on something very expensive, they would call on him to get that spot out.

After Margaret got married, she spent a lot of money on

her clothes, especially when she got ready to go to church. But anytime she'd come out, you really had to stop and look. If you saw her, you would think she'd walked off a calendar and you would say, "That must be Ella Fitzgerald or some big star."

And she could wear hats. Don't care what kind of hat she put on—a little wide or whatever—she looked good in a hat. She wore some of the most beautiful hats that you could ever lay eyes on.

Margaret's husband was a good-looking man and he dressed his tail off too. They were a good match: They both were tall and they wore nice things. He used to love to dance and, oh boy, could he get down. Margaret was in the Eastern Star and she would always be organizing things at their dances. (The Eastern Star is for women and the Masons is for men.) Sometimes, when Margaret was too busy with work, he'd be waiting for me and my friend to come to the dance. Oh, when we get there and that music be playing . . . I danced with him, that tall man. I liked my brother-in-law. Yes, he was a good-looking man.

I've never been jealous of my sisters and brothers. If I had wanted to be jealous, I could've been jealous of Margaret. She's dark with beautiful skin and she wore beautiful things. She knew what to do with herself. Margaret made me look like Salvation Army. I'm not very expensive but I like my things like I like them, you know what I mean? I just dress. I can go out there with dungarees on and get just as many look-ats as you get when you get all dolled up, because they gonna look at you only one time and that's gonna be it. There's nothing more for them to look at. I could've been jealous of Margaret but I wasn't because I had my personality.

Margaret stayed married to her second husband until he died. She was so used to being with somebody that when she lost him it made her halfway uncomfortable. I'm gonna put it that way. She's not crazy or anything like that, but she's uncomfortable because she is not used to being alone. (I can be alone because I've always been alone.) She should have tried to find another guy but she was so much in love with this one. You know, some women are like that. They're so much in love with their husband that if he leaves them, it takes them a long time before they try to hook on to somebody else.

I always say you got to put that love in a little box, like in a little trunk. You're not going to forget but it's just the idea that you are still alive and he is dead. I think you should keep on living for yourself. Get yourself another friend. I'm not saying it's gonna be the same as this one because you were in love with this one. But you can grow to love another one too. I say get another friend but Margaret didn't.

Things got to be different with Margaret. She got to where she wasn't paying too much attention to what she was doing. I'd help her get food in the house, and I used to go down and help her with her banking and stuff like that. I would tell her that we're going to the bank and that I'm gonna be at her house at nine o'clock or ten o'clock in the morning. That would give her plenty of time to get herself up and get herself cleaned up and put some clothes on. I said, "Now when I come, I want you to be ready."

But when I'd get to her house, she'd just be getting out of bed. She'd take ten minutes to put on one shoe and twenty minutes to put on the other shoe. It was getting late, and I knew that she knew that if she kept me away long enough, I'd miss my soaps. She knew I was a soap opera lover and that I wanted to get home in time for them.

I think that Margaret done got to a point where nothing made her too happy. And I think she was trying to bring my happiness down too. I knew what she was doing but I tried to not let it get me. Then when we'd get ready to go to the bank, she would walk slow, real s-l-o-w. I'd say, "Come on, Maggie. Please let's go a little bit faster." Then she'd get on my case and say, "Oh, you . . . you . . . You just always trying to do this and always trying to do that." And I'd say, "No. No. No. No. It's

not like that. I just want us to do what we gonna do." And I'd
ask her, "Where's your bankbook?" She'd say, "I got it." I'd say,
"Well, let me see where it's at." And she'd say, "I told you that
I got it."

Then when we'd get in the bank, she'd have the bankbook
but it wasn't where she could get at it right away. And she'd
say right in front of the bank people, "Where's my bankbook?"
That would make them think that I'm bringing her there to
try to make her get her money out of the bank. I said to her,
"You better be glad you're Momma's child, because I think I
would lose my religion if you wasn't."

Margaret done worry me to death. I would tell her, "Let's
write the slips out in the house before we go." Anybody can
write out a money order on the blank. The date and the number and everything could be written out in advance. Then all
she'd have to do when she got to the bank is go and set and
when the time come for you to get called, all she'd have to do is
go up there and let the tellers see her write her name. Then she
would get the money and that would be it. We could have
done everything before that in the house.

But Margaret didn't want it like that. She wanted to sit
there and let the personnel back there at the desk take care of
that. It just made me sick to my stomach. The people in the
bank were helpful but I know that they'd look at me and think
that I was a damned fool. Why did the bank people have to
write that out for her when I'm there all the time? They'd
think, "Why couldn't her sister do that?" Sometimes when I
got back home, I'd be so washed out with sweat, I'd have to go
and take a bath.

It got so that I had to take her down to the bank one day
and have it all put in my name. Because if anything had gone
wrong with her, nobody would be able to go and get nothing
to pay her rent. So I went down and we got that paper straightened out. From then on, when the time came, I could go and

ask her what she wanted and what she had to pay for the rent and everything. Then I would go to the bank and get the money and bring it back to her: That made more sense.

Margaret went into the nursing home after she had the fire. I believe she set the fire but she never did say that she did. It started in the kitchen of her apartment. The kitchen was the only thing that was burned out; all the cabinets were burned and the floor started burning. She was standing there in the doorway of her apartment and the smoke was coming out. She didn't yell "Fire!" or nothing like that. She was just out of it. I think Margaret set the fire because she was asking for help.

When the firemen came and cooled it off, they had her sitting out there in the hall. She wanted to go back in the apartment. We told the firemen to please call for an ambulance. Margaret wasn't hurt except in her mind. She had a fire and then she had to go into the hospital. Even before the fire she was acting peculiar. After she left the hospital, she needed to have somebody to stay with her. I couldn't stay with her and she just had to have somebody. She didn't have money enough to get somebody to come in so they put her in a nursing home.

The nursing home is in the Bronx. When I go to see Margaret, I have to take two buses. I only go to see her once a week, on Saturday. I don't want them people in the nursing home to think they got somebody coming up there twice a week. Once you start doing it and they get used to it, you know they're looking for you. I don't want them to think they're going to have somebody twice a week to take care of Margaret.

I bring her clothes home and I clean them up and take them back. Sometimes I will go twice a week if I bring home a lot of her clothes and I know she will need them before that next Saturday. I go with the clothes, hand them over, kiss her, love her, and then I leave. I don't want them to get it in their minds that I'm there. I tell them, "This is not a visit. It's just to make sure she has enough clothes to last her until Saturday." And they say, "She's got a nice sister." And I say, "Well, we were taught to love each other."

On Saturday, I stay for three hours. I help Margaret eat; she won't feed herself. I take a biscuit, a roll, whatever they give her, and put butter on it and put it in one of her hands. She'll put it in her mouth and then I'll feed her the rest.

When people get into those places, I don't know what happens to them. Margaret was walking when she went there. Now she can't walk. Her hands were open when she went there. Now she's not using her right hand too well. The left hand she can use some because I make her keep that open. After she was up there for six months, two of her fingers were out and two were digging in. Maybe she had a little arthritis in there, I don't know, but it's not that she broke something. We always put something in her hand because she was beginning to dig a hole down in there. They got something that they can put in her hand to keep her fingers from going in there. It's like they rolled up something like a piece of towel material, like a little pillow. When I go, I talk to her and tell her to open that hand. Seeing your sister like that, it really upsets you.

When Margaret first went to the nursing home, she was hellish. She was so difficult, I thought they were going to tell me that she couldn't stay, but the medicine they gave her calmed her down. She's been there for two years now. There was a time that Margaret wasn't doing anything: She wouldn't turn over; she wouldn't sit up; she wouldn't stand up. They had to lift her out of the bed like they did a bag of potatoes. They had to put a machine under her and hook it in and then screw something and it lifted her out the bed. Then they'd sit her down in the wheelchair. That worried me more than anything else about her there. Before, my sister could've moved a mountain, that's how strong and able she was. And to see her like that . . . it almost killed me.

Margaret used to do everything, things that I didn't think

about doing. But nobody goes to see her in the nursing home. One lady at the church was very good to me when I was trying to get Margaret up there in the nursing home. She helped me with some paperwork to get her up there, and now she goes to visit my sister every once in a while. The deacon in the church comes for the Communion but all them other people that she ran with, nobody comes to see her. Everybody wanted to be bothered with Margaret when she was on her feet but now nobody wants to be bothered.

When Margaret first got up there, the nurses used to say to me, "You know you're very strong. I don't know whether I could stand to see my sister like that." I said, "Honey, that's Momma's child. I can see her any kind of way." And I come, get her in my arms, hold her, and tell her that I love her and try to see if I can make her come back. Margaret's still got me and she's gonna have me. I think Margaret is going to be there when I'm gone, sitting right up there in that nursing home after I'm gone.

Margaret's daughter lives in Brooklyn, but she doesn't go to see her mother. She doesn't bother. Every once in a while I see her, but not too often. We talk on the phone. I just want to keep it like that so we know where she's at. I don't hide anything about how Margaret is. I call her every once in a while and she'll ask a question about her mother. The exact way she puts it is, "How's everybody?" I just say, "Everybody's doing all right." But I don't give her no information unless she asks for it. If she breaks it down and asks me more, I'll give her more. She can go to the nursing home and find out for herself. But she gonna have to make it up in her mind to do it. Then everything will be all right. I feel bad because I have tried. You know, I want everybody to love everybody. I just hope Margaret's daughter don't wait too late.

Julius don't go to see Margaret much because he can't stand to see her like that. He always asks about her. Sometimes when I'm up in the nursing home, I let him talk to her on the telephone. I used to go to Philadelphia but when Margaret took sick, I wasn't gonna leave her here alone. If I leave town and Julius leaves town, Margaret would be there all alone. I don't like it like that. So Julius didn't go: In case somebody called about Margaret, at least he would be around.

I just hope that when I fall by the wayside, somebody will say, "Well, I got to do this for Freddie Mae." And if not, I'm not going to even worry about it because when I was doing it for other people, everything I did, I did from the heart. I didn't do anything because I had to do it or because somebody was paying me to do it. Sometimes you pay people and they still don't do what they're supposed to do. Everything I do, I do it from the heart.

When I go to see my sister Margaret in the nursing home, sometimes I feel so bad for the others out there. They might get visitors through the week or something. I don't know because I'm not out there then. But the way they look is just pitiful. They'll be sitting out there in the hallway and they'll be waving at me. One of them I like very much because her name is Julia, my mother's name. She says, "Hello, Miss Baxter. Hello, Miss Baxter." Every time I go I give her fifty cents just for that name. I say, "I love you because you're named after my mother."

GOD IN MY HEART

Where I grew up, the black kids and the white kids lived near each other. It was more blacks than whites but nobody bothered nobody. We were just neighbors but there was no mixing. (The mixing I'm talking about is like in a restaurant, at a skating rink, in school; those kind of things.) The kids played together but the grown-ups never tried to sit together and have tea or coffee.

Naturally you gonna play with the white kids in the neighborhood. Kids always gonna play. That's why I say if you leave it to the kids, you won't have too much trouble. I think a kid is not selfish unless you make him selfish. Kids always bring somebody home. The black children and the white children did go in each other's houses. If you had to go in somebody's house, you went, and if you didn't have to go, you didn't go. The grown-ups might think about something after you get up in the house and talk about it. Then if the kid asks if he can bring So-and-so home, they might tell him no. If the kids see you never have no blacks in your house, they figure that's the way it's supposed to be.

There was one white girl I played with. Her name was Doris. She really was tough and just like a boy. I could've been about twelve and she could've been about eleven but we were pretty big for our age. She'd act like what they call a butch here in New York, but she never said anything to me. We were young people and it was the thirties. Ain't nobody gonna say nothing. She was tough and I was tough too.

Doris was a good old girl. We would knock around and play ball. We used to shoot marbles. We did a lot of things together. We would tumble; we used to tussle. Her mother and father, they didn't say anything about it because we did it all the time. She would throw me down sometimes, and I would throw her down sometimes. When I would get the best of her, when I had her down on the ground and she knew that I had her, she would call me a name. I'll never forget it. You know what name I mean. She done say something that made me weak. That would bother me so much. When she'd say that, I got so weak in the legs that she could just turn me over and rassle me to death. I should have punched her when she said that. That's what I should've done if I had been as smart as I am now. Today, what she said would mean nothing to me, nothing at all. But at that time, it meant a lot to me. But me and Doris kept in with each other. We didn't fall out.

Down South, the people were more honest than in the North. You always knew what you were doing there. They would say something like, "You gotta know your place." If there was someplace they didn't want you, they'd tell you. They had signs that said COLORED and WHITE and you knew to go in your side. If you went someplace and they didn't want you there, they'd probably step over you.

When I was working, I did my work. When time came for my pay, I got my pay. If I wanted to get on a bus, I got me a seat where I could sit down. If it was in the back, well, that bus was taking me to the same place the front of the bus was taking me. Today, down South things are a lot better: Now you can sit anywhere you want on these same buses.

Way back then—when I say way back, that was in the forties—it was just as bad up North as in the South. If you were on a subway in New York and you wanted to sit down someplace and two white people was coming in, they would try to push you over and beat you to the seat as if it was theirs by right. You'd be getting ready to sit down and somebody would scoot over there first and you'd sit right in their lap. I'm not kidding you. At least we didn't have to go through that in the South. I'd say, "Okay, okay, you can have the seat!" I did all my fighting when I was a kid because I figured that's the way it's supposed to be. But as a grown person, I didn't fight anymore.

Sometimes I go to the mirror and look at myself. I don't mean I'm pretty. But I'm not ugly. I'm not pretty and I'm not ugly. I'm in-between. Let's put it that way. I can pass. I don't call myself light but I mean there's all these different kinds of us.

We're classed as blacks but there's all kind of blacks. We're like a flower garden. There's different colors of us. There's brown. There's light brown. There's a dark brown. There's a black; there's a black black; and there's a light black. You could be called light and another person could be called light but each of them lights is different. You can just see it in the person. I can see the difference. I'm not blind. I can see who is who. But in the family, we didn't figure it that way; who was darker or who was lighter.

I consider myself brown. Margaret is dark brown—I would call it—because she's darker than me. Julius is the darkest. He's much darker than me and Margaret. Victoria was the lightest of all of us. I was the next brownest to her. My mother was about Margaret's complexion, a little darker than I am. My older brother, Bill, he was a dark brown. He was in between me and Margaret.

Years ago, it used to be that the lighter girls would always get the boyfriends. In my day, the little light girls, they always got the hugs from the little boys. When I was coming up back there, the little boys just liked the little light girls. We didn't say light girls back then. We used to call them yaller girls. It looked like the boys figured they were prettier. Today, it's not like that. It looks like the blackest the berry, the sweeter the juice. I know that little black girls get just as many boyfriends as the little yaller girls ever did.

One way a colored person is different from a white person is the colored person might say, "You know I was in some place and everybody was looking at me." You could never hear me say that. I could go anyplace and I don't know whether you're looking at me or not. Because I walk in and whatever I'm gonna do, I do. If I'm gonna buy something, I buy something. And I'm not gonna look to see whether you're looking at me. 'Cause if you're looking, I wouldn't know it unless I'm looking at you.

I don't have no color, like I like this one better than that one. I'll grab and kiss you just as quick as I would kiss one of my sisters. I don't have any color. I just love people. 'Cause God put people in this world, on this earth, to love each other. Black people are afraid of white people and white people are afraid of us. I don't mean hitting somebody in the head. You're scared that I'm gonna be nasty if you come up to me and approach me. I think if I come up and approach you, you're gonna be nasty. Nobody knows what the other is gonna do. That's the way they pull a line between us and keep pulling. That line keeps pulling and stretching and stretching. People are willing to think somebody's going to do something to you. Now I know that people do dirty deeds, but everybody doesn't do a dirty deed, everybody is not mean.

Everybody talks about who likes who, like you don't like black and I don't like white. Some people look for respect but they don't know how to get it. If you give it, I swear to God, you'll get it. I declare they might not do it today but they gonna do it tomorrow or the next day. But if you be mean and I be mean, how in the hell are we going to embrace each other or shake each other's hand? Somebody's got to give.

I don't know anything about slavery but what I read. Remember *Roots,* that colored picture they made? What the kids saw on TV made them want to do things to people that they shouldn't do. These kids see that and sometimes what you see is what you do. They see that the white people were beating the colored so they get where they just don't have respect for nobody. Some people now would cut your whole arm off just to get your ring. That's what the TV show made them do when they saw what they did to the colored people back there.

That show got the kids thinking that everybody is like they were, when their great-great-great-grandfather and their great-great-great-grandmother were coming up. The people that did the beating then, them old people that are dead back there, they've been gone so long that they are strangers, all strangers to the ones that's alive today. They've been gone too long for you to blame their offsprings. Because now it's not those old people's children, it's their children's children's children. And they didn't do anything. People cannot be responsible for what their great-great-grandparents did. It was wrong, what the ancestors did, but I don't see why this generation's got to suffer for it.

The kids who saw the TV show are not living because they're thinking about what them dead people back there did. But they should be saying to themselves, "Now, why should I be mean like this for something that happened four hundred years ago? Those people that were hurt are dead and buried; they ain't coming back to help you." I say, "Heal yourself and build." That's all I want. If I had anything to do with it, I would tell them, "Just heal. Please. Please. Do that for me."

I don't care who says I'm wrong. I have to think for myself. This country is off track. We need to get the country back on track. Some of the wheels are on the track but they've got to put the other wheels on there for that train to run. Somebody needs to say something besides sending a rocket to the moon. If you can't live on earth, how you gonna live on the moon? You don't know them little people on the moon. You got to heal and if you don't, you ain't never gonna be right.

You lose lots of energy and your health, worrying about what happened in 1888. You're killing your health, you know. Ain't nobody here from that time. So who are you mad at? Those people that's dead over there now, you can't be mad at them. They're gone. You are living here on this earth. You should give these kids a chance to live. Let something come along and make these people heal where you can live the balance of your days without all this hatred in you. It's just like that glass of milk that's spilled and you can't get it back.

You can't just sit up and be angry all the time, because you're gonna die before you get anything straightened out. And then there's gonna be another generation coming up with anger and they're gonna die too before they get straightened out. These kids I'm talking about are not helping themselves. They have a right to be angry. But I say, "Be angry and build." Go ahead and be angry. Be angry as much as you want but while you are angry, build from all that anger you got. You can take a few of our people and put it together and make something of it. We could get together but nobody's being the one that wants to do that. That's why I wish I could get something or head something and probably start it off. I want people to heal and build. I just want them to live right.

The Jews really did heal themselves. Lots of Jews got killed—like you would kill a roach or something—and they were pushed in trenches and in camps. But they came and rose above it. That's what made me feel good about the Jewish people. Right today, if there's a Jewish holiday, all the stores are closed. You can hardly buy in no place. You see what the Jews did. They believe you take your money and put it all together and build something for yourself.

You know, way back in Florida, they used to do the Jews kind of bad. They didn't want them in here or they couldn't go in there. I knew about this woman who went to Florida with her child. And while she was down there in this hotel they didn't treat her right. They didn't want her to be there. And she came back to New York and later went back down to Florida and she bought that hotel. Now that's what you call building. You build from your anger. When I heard that story, oh, did I clap my hands. And I said, "That's so beautiful."

You'd be surprised how people stick together when there's a crisis, like when we had the big blackout in New York in 1977. Let's say a storm or something comes along and destroys a whole lot of stuff. You'd be so glad to lean on my arm or let me pet you. I'd be so glad to lean on your arm. Why do we have to wait until disaster comes to be so kind to each other? You're always trying to get something that costs you money. Kindness is something that don't cost you a dime.

My mother went to church and she made us go. It was a Baptist church. I was baptized there but it wasn't because I wanted to be. Even as a child, I never did like church. I went because I had to. If I didn't go, I would get beat. I promised that if I ever got grown, church wouldn't be one of my things.

It came to me when I was a little girl. I was thinking: Why do the preacher ride when we got to walk? You know you're walking to church and the hot sun out there is coming down on you. Down South, the sun is worse; when it gets hot and you're walking, you can see diamonds in front of your face. Now when the preacher comes to church, if he's not in a car, he's in a buggy. He's got something over him to cover him up. But I'm walking out there. And the sole of my shoe is coming off. I had to take an ice pick and bore some holes in my shoe and then take the smallest hairpin and put that wire in to hold that sole on my shoe. If you didn't fix it, you'd go flip-flap, flip-flap. The preacher's children got shoes, the right kind of shoes. They ain't flapping.

Ever since I was a little girl, I'm thinking: Why does it have to be like that? Why does the preacher got to have this? Why does the preacher have to have anything? Why has he got a better-looking house than anybody else? And you got to take up money, too, to send the preacher on a vacation. I just made it up in my mind then that you can make me go to church now, but you ain't going to be able to make me go when I get grown, because I'm not going.

In our town, our preacher had a roller-skating rink for his grandkids. All the other kids used to come and pay a dime or so and get skates; then they could go and skate. Well, the church decided that he shouldn't have that because he was the pastor of the church. And it wasn't a white man either that did it, that made him give the skating rink up. The church people felt he shouldn't have a thing that children could come to and have a good time. We had something to keep us happy but they made him give it up. He didn't have it for himself; he had grandkids that he had that for. It couldn't have been because he was charging money; he was only charging ten cents. But they made him give it up, and we were out of that. That's what made me angry. That's why I don't believe in them church people. The white kids still had a skating rink and we couldn't go to theirs because we didn't mix.

On Sunday when you go to church, you hear what the preacher says. He'll be sitting up there and preaching and praying. He says he's gonna do this or that for the church but nothing never gives. Next Sunday, it's the same story. And you'll put your little fifteen or twenty cents on the table and he grabs it up. That money goes to the preacher. Today, when they're taking up the collection in church, they don't want your change. They say, "No noisy money. No noisy money."

They want your paper money. They're begging but you got to give them what they want. If it was me, I'd be just as satisfied if somebody put a five-cent piece or a quarter in my collection plate.

Another thing that gets me is that the preacher can get up on that pulpit and preach all he wants to preach and you believe him. But I don't go to church to hear all that preach, preach, preach. 'Cause what they say there, I know. I know what he knows.

I won't go to church and I don't hide it but I'll go to a church function if somebody has something and I think I might like it, like a concert where there's gonna be lots of singing. I've got friends who go to church every Sunday or every other Sunday but I stay right in my house on Sunday unless there's something I want to do on the outside. But I believe in God. Nobody has never seen God. We don't know who He is but we still pray. I pray every night for my family and my friends. And He hears me just like He hears the ones that go to church every Sunday or every other Sunday. I believe in God. Nobody can take that away from me. I bet you any amount of money that I'll get up there to heaven just as fast as them that go to church every Sunday because I have it in my heart. There's some people that swear they love the church so much. They go, go, go there but they would never do the things that I would do to help somebody, to be even nice to somebody. I think that if you are in the church, you should be able to be nicer than I would be.

I go visit a friend in a nursing home that's near me. The nurse is trying to make her talk. She asks her, "Who is this lady?" My friend says, "Freddie Mae Baxter." The nurse says, "Is this your sister? Is this your cousin? Is this your so-and-so-and-so?" And she says, "No. It's a very good Christian friend." Now I'm not a Christian; I don't go to church. But that's what she said. I didn't say, "No, I'm not." I just let it go.

I know I'm not a Christian but I love. If you love somebody, you've got God in your heart. Christianity comes from love. If you ain't got nothing in your heart, you can forget it. That's what love is all about. You can get out and say, "I love you. I love you. I love you," but that don't mean anything if it's not in your heart.

KEEPING UP WITH THE DEAD

I can see really clearly in my dreams. I could tell what happens and it could be almost like a five-page letter. You know, all those things when you're dreaming.

What really gets me is when I dream about money, like a large sum of money under my pillow. That dream is so real that when I wake up, I really look under the pillow to see if it's there. How I would love for that to happen.

One time, I was working for a family and they had a bookcase in their house with a desk, one of those big units they have where you could put books, a video, or whatever, and you could sit there and do your writing. I dreamed about the father in that family after he died. I dreamed he had put some money away there and he told me it was behind that unit. The way my dream was telling it, the money was in stacks, like you see it in the bank with little paper around them—in fifties or hundreds. The next time I went to work, the first thing I did was to look behind that unit. I really did go there and look behind it. I didn't have to move the furniture. There was a hollow back there that I could peek through. But the money wasn't there. I know it was a dream but if it had been there, I would have told the family about it. I would not have kept it to myself. I said, "Lord, have mercy. Why couldn't this dream have been true?"

. . .

Sometimes a dream can be so real, you could swear to God that it really happened. I had a very awful dream the other night. We were at the 125th Street station of the railroad. This little girl was there, about ten or eleven years old. She was going around the station and bothering people for money. She came up to me. I had a handful of change and it was in a tray like you put your money in when you get change. Well, she picked in my tray and got some of the money out. I said, "Wait! What are you doing? You stop that!" I said to her, "Don't ever do that again." She went down the platform a little further and she start picking at an old lady. So I went up to her and said, "You stop picking at that old lady." The little girl started to run and I started running after her. She jumped out there where the train was and she kept running on the tracks. I was right behind her but I was on the platform, running until I could get to the end of the platform. And I said, "Oh, my God. Why is that child down there?" She had decided to cross the track. After the train passed, I was looking for her to be on the other side but the train hit her. I didn't see her anymore. That train done hit her. I knew it hit her, because she went across the tracks. It woke me up about five. I was really disturbed. I thought it was my fault: If I hadn't been running out there, she wouldn't be running across there. I said, "Why did I run after that little child . . . ?" Then I went back to sleep and dreamed about something else.

Sometimes I fly in my dreams. I remember one time I was flying and the people wanted everybody to be on dope. And they got everybody they could find to be on it and they were after me and a friend of mine. I picked her up and started flying with her and they were shooting needles at us, you know hypodermic needles. They were using bows and arrows to shoot at us and they shot her. She told me to drop her and to go ahead on because they done got her. But I wouldn't. And I was getting away, flying across the telephone wires. I tell you, I achieved something.

When I was in my early thirties, quite a ways back, I dreamed about my mother. She was a younger person. I dreamed she had left home to come up North (which she had never really done when she was alive). When she came back, she looked so good; she was all dressed up, but she was acting like she was too high up to talk to us. She wasn't angry. She didn't say, "Get out of there" or nothing like that. She just didn't want to be my mother. And I was saying, "Momma, you're my momma." But she didn't want to talk, and I started crying. That particular night, I was so upset, I woke up and said to myself, "Oh, my God. Why didn't she want to say that she was our mother?"

I dreamed a dream about our father too. He wanted to be the father and I was telling him no. He said, "I am your father." And I said, "No. No. No. No." That was a dream where I didn't care whether I dreamed it or not. When I woke up, I was looking around. I said if this was really true, I'm talking to myself.

One time in a dream, me and Margaret had a big argument. I told you how Momma never did like for us to argue and fight, how she wanted us to be kind to each other. In this dream my mother came to me and I could feel her on the back of my bed. She spoke with me and said for me and Margaret to get back together again. She said, "Don't be fighting and carrying on like that." The next morning I called Margaret and said, "I was dreaming about Momma last night. And it seems like you and I got in a big fight and Momma told me she wanted for us to be kind to each other."

And then two or three weeks later, me and Margaret did get in an argument. This is for real now. I got so mad I told her that I wasn't going to be bothered with her anymore, that I wasn't gonna talk to her. Then another thing happened. My brother-in-law James, Lumisha's husband, came up from the South. He said he wanted to see us in Rockaway Beach, where he was visiting his sister. He came and he wanted to see us. And he was somebody that I loved to death.

Well, it was just like Momma sent him: It was almost like he was a messenger. Something kept pushing me and pushing me. I said to myself, "He's Margaret's brother-in-law too. Maybe he wants to see her too." So I called Margaret and I asked her to go. Me and Julius and her, we went out to Rockaway. Do you know that me and her started talking and we ain't got in no argument since. Momma sent Lumisha's husband here. And I don't care what nobody says, I know she sent him.

Looks to me now like every time somebody hurt me, my mother comes when I'm dreaming. If I get upset, she comes to me, so help me God. I remember one time she came, I could actually feel it, as if she was back there behind me. She had me in her arms and she held me. I felt something around me just like I was hugging myself. I know it was a dream but I could really feel it. She was talking and talking to me and consoling me.

I want to see my mother but I wish she would just come for a friendly visit, come and sit with me for a while, you know. I want it to be a pleasant thing that me and her just talk. I would like to be laughing with her. I'm not afraid when she comes. It's a funny thing: My mother's been dead almost sixty years, but when I talk about her, I talk just like she died yesterday or the day before.

I just have all kinds of dreams. And some are so true, I really feel that it happened. I have gone to my mother's funeral in a dream. I could see her laying up in there just as big as daylight. I have gone to my mother's funeral and heard the kids saying and my friends saying, "Freddie Mae, I'm sorry to hear that your mother passed." This dream is a dream I only have now, not back there when she died.

Years ago, an older person told me that the dead people are not gonna let you see them go away. Because if you see them, they probably want you to follow them. So if the dead people are talking to you, they'll say, "Would you get me a glass of water?" And you go and get it, and then when you come back to give it to them, they're gone. My mother never did let me see her leave. Like she'll be talking to me and we'll be walking through a tunnel and you can see the light at the end of the tunnel. When we get almost there, my mother says, "Ohhhh." And when I look back, she's gone. She did that for me not to go there. She never let me go out of that tunnel.

Sometimes you could dream that a light be up in the ceiling. And for heaven's sake, you can pull that cord, you can turn the switch, and that light will not come on. Every light switch I touch, it just won't click on. All I do is hear it click. But there is no light.

I was talking to my brother Julius about it. He says that the reason why you can't pull the light on is maybe they don't mean for you to know whatever it is that you're dreaming about. Julius says, "Maybe if you pull the light on, you might see something you're not supposed to see."

I'm not easily frightened by things that God takes care of but one time I saw something from out my window that scared me to death. The driveway to my house is like a horseshoe, like the cars come in there and come around. Inside that horseshoe, in that circle there's grass, hedges around, and trees. About six years ago, I happened to see a bright light in my room and I didn't know what it was. I'm laying up in my bed in the middle of the night and the moon was in my yard, just like if a balloon would come right out that window and sit up there. And it was shining bright as day. It was right out there, bright as bright can be and shining on me. I'm on the twelfth floor of my building and the moon was right there. It wasn't way up in the air now, not way up. If it had been way over, I wouldn't have been frightened. I'm not a person to get frightened so fast. But my heart could've jumped right out of my body. I said, "Now why would that moon be right there?" But it was too close. If it had come down any further, it could've been right there in the yard where the trees was. If it had come down, it would've dropped right in that circle there.

My girlfriend was staying over that night, and she saw it too. She was on the couch and I was in the bed. I said to her, "Hey, hey," very quiet; she was as frightened as I was. I got up and we went to the window and there it was out there. I turned my head and wouldn't look anymore. I don't know why I was scared but I was frightened to death. I just turned my back and tried to stop thinking what that sign could mean, and I got back in bed.

Friday the 13th don't bother me. The only thing that bothers me is if I'm going someplace and I see a black cat getting ready to walk across my path. A long time ago, they used to talk about that and they always said that it was bad luck. When I see a black cat, I turn all the way around and go the other way. It has happened to me but not too often because there ain't too many cats out there. I don't know what happened to them but thank God we don't have too many cats running around in New York City now.

I never walk on manhole covers. I don't care where I am, I'll walk around them every time. I was in Philly one year and a little boy fell down there and they never found him. I believe there's alligators under the streets. I guess they ate him. Every time I called my family in Philly, I would try to ask them, "Was anything in the papers about the little boy?" And there wasn't. You can go down one of them manholes and there ain't no coming back. So any time I see one of them manhole covers, I walk around it! I don't care where I am.

Years ago, I used to be scared of dead people. When you go to a wake, you can see the person unless they're in a bad condition, like they could have got killed in an accident. Then they won't let you see the body but they put their picture up there on the casket. But long as they just died of natural things heart attack, you have the whole body there that you can ͺ

I used to have bad experiences with that. If I would go tͺ the undertaker and the people that died be laying this way, I tried to make sure when I get home that I turn my bed around and I lie the other way. I didn't want to lay the same way that they were laying because I could've dreamed about them and I'm gonna see them laying there.

When I'd go home, I could see them all night that night, either coming through the door or coming through the window or sitting in my chair. When they were in the room with me, they were dressed just like they wasn't dead. They was just themselves, and they wanted to talk. That's what got me. They talked and they wanted to ask me questions. I talked to them, but I didn't want to. I was too scared to say "Go away," because they were themselves and they wanted to talk. I used to be so frightened, I'd wake up soaking wet.

Now nothing bothers me anymore. I stopped being scared of dead people. I can go see three or four that same day and come home and just sleep, sleep, sleep. I think that taking care of funerals in my family changed me. I had to go and tell them what I wanted them to put on, how I wanted the hair fixed, and make sure they have powder and lipstick and everything like that. I'm just not scared anymore. I don't know whether it's because I got a little closer to the Man Up There. That's why I tell you that nobody can be so sick that I can't go and see them. You might say, "Oh, I just can't stand this." But I can take anything now. I think I got a little closer to Him, that's all.

There's this girl . . . The only time we see each other is when somebody from our hometown dies. They're our people but they're all up here in New York now. When they die, all I got to do is call her. Then she and I, we call, and get everybody up to the funeral. And you see people you haven't seen in twenty, sometimes thirty years.

h dead people. I got a book where I put down
body when they die. It's just something that
. I must've started it in 1953 when I wanted
ᴅown when my mother and my sister died. I said from
now on, every time somebody died, I'm going to put it in here.
White people, black people, blue, green, Chinese, whatever;
movie stars and different things . . . When they die and they're
in the newspaper, I put it down in my book.

I just put in their name, when they died, and how old they
were when they died. That's all. I don't get the whole story.
When somebody dies, there's not so much that you can get
out. I just have a line for each person. I don't want to know
anything else about them because if I liked them good enough,
I'd just cut the picture out of the paper and keep it. And I'd
put their picture in another book.

It's a thick little book like a notebook, like the kind you
would buy for a child to take to school. I just have a line for
each person. When I first started, I was skipping two lines but
it got so heavy there, I had to use some of the lines that I was
skipping.

If I like them or don't like them, I put them in the book
because I want to remember. I got Ella Fitzgerald and Billie
Holiday. They only thing I can't catch up with is when Billie
Holiday died. I got it when she was born and everything but I
don't have when she died. I'm going to catch it one of these
days. You know they're going to be talking on the radio and
they might say when Billie Holiday died. But she's the only
one. Everyone else I've got. I've got not just musicians but
other people. All the people back there with Shirley Temple,
like the five little girls that were born at that time. I think
three of them are dead and two of them are alive. I got Mel
Allen down. When Billy Martin was killed, I got that down. I
write about everybody. (When I'm doing something, I'm

doing it.) I got so many white people in my book, it's not even funny: People died here like flies not too long ago.

My friends and I, we'll get in a conversation and when somebody comes up and say, "Can you remember what year So-and-so died in?" I don't have to think. I can just go to my book and find the name.

I don't love no dead people. I do not love you if you are dead, because I can't do anything for you. You can't hear anything I say. You can't feel anything. Now you might say if somebody died in my family and I'm not doing any crying, she must've been an awful sister. Because I do not cry over no dead people. I loved them when I could love them, when they let me love them. But when they're dead, they can't love me and let me love them so I don't do it. I say: Don't give a person your love when they are dead, because they don't need it.

Don't get me wrong. If you die now, don't say I didn't love you. I love like everybody else because everybody can love. You and I had a good time together but I don't die because you die. I am not going when you go 'cause I ain't dead. Like Moms Mabley, the comedian lady, says, "Now you dead. Not me." And that's the way I am too.

Some people want to love you only when you're dead. Those people are the ones that do all the hollering. They almost pull you out of the casket, saying, "Ohhh, Daddy!" That don't make sense. You give him love when he is alive.

That person laying up there could've used your help for a bath. Or she could've used your help to get her hair washed. She could've used your help to wash her feet and maybe cut her toenails or something. But you wouldn't come and do that. You wouldn't come and do anything.

You're supposed to do for me while I'm alive. But you didn't come to help me get a bath when I couldn't do it for myself. Then I die and you're going to try to pull me out of the casket because you love me so much. You don't love me. Them people that didn't do anything, they're going to come when you die. And when you die, when you're laid up there in the casket, they want to come and pull you out. You don't need them now. What do you need them for?

Let's say that you die and some money is left. Most of the time the person that dies will leave somebody's name on something and they'll get it all settled. But that's not what I'm talking about. When you die, everybody comes out. You'll find you have all kinds of cousins and all kinds of nieces and they say, "She thought I should have had this or I should have had that." Why couldn't all these nieces and cousins come when this person needed them?

My sister Margaret is different from me. She could worry about a dead person but I could not worry about a dead person. My brother Julius would be the only one I could say that if anything happened to him, it would really knock me for a loop. We're so close that it just really would get me. We love and cherish each other. We don't have to worry about that in death 'cause we doing it now. He depends on me a great deal and I depend on him a great deal. If he is dead, what can I do for him? I can't do anything for him anymore. And why should I make myself sick over him. He wouldn't want that to happen to me. He would want me to go ahead on and live. If it happened to me, I would want the same thing for him.

Julius said if he should go, he wanted to be cremated, but I talked him out of it. I said, "I really would like to have you buried but if I can't talk you into it and being cremated is what you really want, I will do it, because I'm not going to let you come back here and mess around with me." I said, "If I did something you said you didn't want done, you could come back and worry me. If I do what you say, you ain't gonna be coming back and no dead will be bothering me." If he still wanted it, I'd do what he says. But, I told him, "I would really like to have you buried." After I talked to him like that, he said, "Okay. If you still alive, you gonna be the one over it anyway, so whatever you do, I accept." I hugged him and kissed him because that's what I wanted. You're dead anyway so being cremated is not going to bring you back and is not going to take you any further.

I'm not afraid to die. I'm really not afraid. I used to be when I was younger. Now I got it all planned. If my doctor says I have a terminal disease, something that can't be cured, I'm going to take care of everything myself. You know if I just die, I can't do nothing about it. But if I have some months, then I can think about it. Let's say I got about six months to live or a year or something like that, I would go to the undertaker, let him show me the books of the caskets, and I'd choose what I want.

If anything happens to me, I want everybody to look at me. I'm going to be one of the most beautiful corpses you ever laid eyes on. You know some people can really fix you up in those caskets. Don't let nobody fool you. I'm gonna leave here with the cutest little smile on my face that you ever laid eyes on. I want to have that smile because I enjoyed myself while I was here. I hope that everyone at the funeral will be smiling too. I don't want them to come in there and do no hollering over me. I don't want them crying, because I know we had a good time when I was alive. Crying ain't gonna bring me back. I just want them to look at me and smile and say, "Goodbye, my friend" or "Goodbye, my sister" or "Goodbye, Auntie."

I told my friends to get up and sing for me and talk about me. The church people ain't gonna say nothing about me, because I don't go to church. I'll have my funeral in the undertaker's. And I say the song that you sing, make sure it's a happy song. There's one song that I really want them to sing for me. It's "Just a Closer Walk with Thee."

I've got a girlfriend who I've been knowing some fifty-odd years. I tease her a lot. I tell her she can't sing but she really does pretty good. Sometimes when I'm talking at the card table, I say, "You know when I die, I want them to sing the song 'Just a Closer Walk with Thee,' but I don't want you to sing it." Those people cracked up and she cracked up but she knows that she's one of my friends. She knows that I love her. And she just laughed. I might even talk my niece Carol into singing it. I told the family when the time comes to bury me, all they have to do is sign the paper and everything is gonna be all ready. All they got to do is put me in there.

When somebody dies, I don't think you should spend a lot of money to bury that person. You could put somebody in a five-thousand-dollar or a six-thousand-dollar casket but do you know for sure whether they put that casket you paid for in the ground or not? You have to leave the cemetery before they do that, before they let that casket go down. The family and everybody has to leave. So you don't know that it's the same casket. It really bugs me to see how people can be so tricky.

I don't have a plot of land set aside for myself. Some of my family is buried in Butler, New Jersey. Margaret's husband is in there. I couldn't be buried over Bubba because Daisy is buried over him. That's all of our family that's in there. If Julius doesn't get married to somebody and if I don't wind up and find me a rich man and get married, we might be buried there. Like if I go before him, he might be buried on top of me. If he goes before me, I might be buried on top of him.

I'm really not scared to die. I think about it all the time. Because we're all going whether you want to go or you don't want to go. One of these days, all of us are going. We're all leaving the same way, whether you were assassinated or whether you were killed or whether you just died, you're still dead. You might just die a natural death or you might go out there, fall down, and hit your head on the sidewalk. I know people who went overseas in the army; they shot guns and fought the war. Then they came back home, stubbed their toe, fell on the ground, hit their head, and died. We never know when it's gonna happen. That's one thing you don't have any say-so about. I don't care what the doctor does or what the doctor says. If that's your number, the doctor can't do anything about it. God may let the doctor take care of you and keep you going at that time but God has you in his hand. Now you know I'm not a church person, but when I can't talk with anybody else, I can talk to Him. When I'm out walking and I cross the street to get over to the other side, I say, "Thank you." Something might happen to you just like that, where you don't even have a chance to say, "Lord have mercy." You can never know when you're in the right place or the wrong place, so it's good to say "Thank you" while you can.

When we were coming up as young people, we could play all the music we wanted. We could play all the old songs. We could take a comb and put a piece of wax paper on it. (When we couldn't get wax paper, we used our notebook paper that we write on.) You can make some beautiful music with a comb. And I used to mess around with a tin tub too, drumming on it. When I was a kid, I didn't play real music but I used to mess around with it.

We had another thing, called a juice horn. It was made of tin and looked like a cigar. It cost a nickel or a dime. You had to blow in it but not with the fingers working. You just blew in it. And I loved to hear the guitar. When I was about ten or eleven, you could always find a man in my neighborhood who wanted to hit on a guitar. We used to play all the old songs. Some of us danced and some of us played and we would really raise sand.

I didn't play a musical instrument until I came up North. When I first got to New York, I heard an all-girl group play. They were named the Sweethearts of Rhythm and they were really good. There was one girl there who played the saxophone that could make you lay down and want to die. I thought that playing the saxophone must really be a kick. I saw that a girl playing a big old horn like that was really something and I wanted to play something that would make people really look at me. So I went 'round to find me a teacher to talk to. In those days, you could go down Forty-seventh Street and see lots of signs saying TEACHER FOR SO-AND-SO. I was walking down the street and saw a sign for a saxophone teacher so I went in. The man's name was Walter Thomas and he was the saxophone player in the Cab Calloway band.

He said if I could get a horn, he would teach me. He had a music school up in Harlem. I went there a couple of times but I didn't like it. I didn't want to be with a whole lot of other people. I wanted my lessons to be private so he could hang over my shoulder and make me learn. If I missed something, he could tell me right away. That way, I'd learn much faster. I paid him five dollars a lesson, which was a lot of money at the time. He taught me well, and I studied with him for quite a spell. He had a few girl groups he was teaching and he told me that he wanted me to go and play with them. He was the one who set me up to play with all-girl groups. I spent quite a few years learning music and rehearsing and I still could have learned some more. You don't ever learn enough when you're playing music.

When I was out playing for people, I'd get just as much enjoyment from it as I believe they got. I used to really blow my horn. When I had to blow them low notes, people just had to listen because I went down there and got them. You know I don't just play. I read music. I can read most anything in saxophone music. I do more reading than playing it by ear. Everybody in the band had to read; there was no ad-libbing. You had to read because if you're not reading it, you're going to hit a wrong note and it's going to stand out. You know a bad note always stands out.

When you play by ear, you can only play so much. But when you read music you can play anything. We played classical music, dance music. I enjoyed playing, so it didn't matter whether it was concert music or dance music. I played in dif-

ferent bands. One was a small six-piece band that was a dance
group. That was two trombones, my tenor saxophone, piano,
drums, and guitar. The two trombones were husband and wife.
(The husband was the leader of the band.) And I played plenty
of solos. There was always a solo in there for me. We played
together for about four years. We really used to have some kind
of fun. We just jammed, and we played everything in those
days. One band I played in was a concert band. Sometimes it
could be as high as thirteen or fourteen pieces. Sometimes it
could be two tenor sax, two alto sax, the piano, two trum-
pets—sometimes three—then the drums and the bass.

Playing concert music really did teach me how to read
music. I'd just sit back there with my horn and read that stuff.
I could play Bach; we played a piece by Beethoven. We had to
play all that music and I hated it. Some people like a concert
but I don't like it. I like dance music. I got more out of the
dance stuff than I got out of the concert. I would say to myself
that if this was jazz, I would be just bouncing off the floor. I
don't like concert music, but I still played it because I wanted
to be in the band.

I like dance music. I like music that you can slow dance by
especially. I can listen to it all day and all night. That's just
how much I love it. But like I said before, the only music I
don't like is opera. I don't like to listen to it and I don't like to
play it. Opera is very hard to play, and it's not my kind of
music. But a lot of people love opera. The place is just as
crowded as a jazz place.

In almost every band I was in, a man was the leader, but in
one band, a lady was the leader, and that was great. She took
care of everything. When we went out, the money was shared.
We didn't make much money like the groups that are going
around today: There wasn't no money out there in the forties
and fifties. I had to have another job for real money, but this
was fun—and we made a little bit, too.

In the band where the leader was a lady, we played all the

Hawaiian music that I enjoyed. I don't know why she wanted that Hawaiian music but we played quite a bit of it. I loved that music. It's so soothing. You feel like you're just waving around. When we played it, everybody was blowing their horns. My favorite piece was "Sweet Leilani." I would love to go to Hawaii, where they wear those skirts and them guys are eating fire.

The bands I was with sometimes played outside the city, at little clubs in New Jersey. I wouldn't travel further than that. Some of the girls traveled because they'd ride airplanes. A lot of them went overseas playing in bands. I said, "No airplanes for me. If I can't get where I'm going on a bus or a car, I'm not going." I just won't ride airplanes; I never have and never will.

The girls I played with in the bands, we didn't hang out together too much but we knew where each other was if we wanted to call. Sometimes we would meet in the clubs or at the dances. Anyplace that there was music, you could find me. I used to hang around with the musicians that were playing. The white guys used to come up and play with them in the after-hours joints in Harlem. Sometimes I would join them, and sometimes I'd sit up in my house alone enjoying myself just blowing my horn.

I wanted to play the saxophone because I used to think that anybody can play the piano, that it was for little people. But I wish now that I had learned the piano because I have the fingers for it. Well, I'm not going to even worry about it now. I played what I played—a little of the drums too: the bongos.

To get someplace in music, you have to do so many things for the leader or the head of it or whatever, just to get in there, that maybe you don't even want to do. Girls in music don't get in there just because they're real good. Those fellas make them do things that they shouldn't do. You have to do lots and I wouldn't do it.

If you say no to them, you just don't play. I was out there

and I heard how fellas would ask the girls for different things. And I said, "No, it ain't going to be like that." I knew I was not ever going to get anywhere if I had to do something I didn't want to do just to be able to play my horn that I done went to school for. I said I didn't think I would ever get famous if they had to use me to get me up there. I knew I would never get no place, but just stay on the bottom. And once you get up there, maybe you will turn around and try to make somebody else do something to get as high up there as you. If I had said yes and done what a man wanted, I might have messed my career up.

Believe me when I tell you that when I do it, it's going to have to be because I want to do it. I have my own mind. Nobody can ever say, "I made Freddie Mae do this" or "I did this to Freddie Mae." If I want to, I will. If I don't want to, I won't. I just don't do what somebody else wants me to do unless I decide that's what I want to do.

I didn't have no problems. I was in a concert group with older people. Then I was in a dance group with an older guy and a younger one. I don't mind being around an old man. You know an old man is gonna do but so much to you. The best he can do is pat you. An older man has a lot in his head for talking but when it comes to acting, down there is different.

I think all of them people I played with are gone now. I'm the only one that I know is alive. I know the piano player is dead; the guitar player is dead; the two trombones are dead. And I wasn't the youngest one. The drummer was really much younger than me. Oh, he was a pretty boy. I shouldn't say he is dead, because I don't know. He'd have to be about sixty now. I don't know whether I would remember him or not, that was so long ago.

I like the music of lots of people. I was crazy about Billy Eckstine, and I was crazy about little Jimmy Scott who done got old now but he's still working. I liked Count Basie. I liked Duke Ellington. I liked quite a few of the white bands too:

Tommy Dorsey, Jimmy Dorsey, Harry James. For years, we danced by the music of Count Basie, Duke Ellington, Glenn Miller, and the two brothers, Jimmy and Tommy Dorsey. I used to sit up and just dance by their music. I would dance and dance.

My favorite was Glenn Miller. His stuff was so mellow and I loved to dance to it. He was just all right. My second-favorite band was Benny Goodman. Now I liked all the rest of them but those two were just so good.

Glenn Miller, he was supposed to have gotten killed in an air force plane. When I heard he was dead, I cried and said, "There's not going to be any more good music." But his band still went on. Somebody took it over but it ain't ever been the same. Just like Duke Ellington, he died back there not too long ago and his son took over. I think Duke Ellington's grandson got the band now.

"Stardust" was my piece. It's one of the prettiest pieces in the world. I love that piece anytime they play it. Hoagy Carmichael was the one that wrote it, but for the musician I like Coleman Hawkins to play it. When he plays it, honey I'm gone.

When I used to go to dances, I didn't stay in one place. I'd see a whole lot of people. When "Stardust" was playing, if anybody came up to ask me to dance, I'd say, "No, thank you," because that was one piece I wouldn't dance with anybody in the dance hall but the guy I went there with. I don't care who asked me for a dance, when "Stardust" came on, that was his. I didn't care whether it was the last piece or the first piece or the in-between piece; I made it my business to get back there to where he was.

Years ago, we used to come over to New York from Jersey to go to the Paramount and the Strand theaters. We heard Frank Sinatra when he was starting out and we thought he couldn't sing. He was a young guy at the time. (His first child,

Nancy, had just been born.) And he was so thin. We used to go see him in New York and we would yell and holler, "You can't sing. You can't sing." And we did little stupid things. We'd throw different things, like soda cans, at his picture on the billboard up there. You know, that guy died a millionaire. He had the money and I ain't got a pot and I ain't got a window to throw it out of. I really like Frank Sinatra's singing now. The guy sings so beautifully. But when he started out, I didn't like him at all.

I liked Peggy Lee when she sang "Fever . . . fever all through the night." I liked all those old-timers. They used to be nice, but then they got so fat. Remember how thin Rosemary Clooney used to be? I'd walk all day long before I let myself get all bloated out like that unless I get sick and it happens. I liked Ella Fitzgerald but she just wasn't one of my favorites. I liked Dinah Washington and I liked Aretha Franklin. I liked Gladys Knight and the Pips.

My favorite singer of all singers is Billie Holiday. I just love my Billie. To me, she sang better than anybody. That woman, I swear to God, I could actually hold her in my arms. That's how much I cared for her. Sometimes I would be in the house by myself and I used to sit down and put all her records on the machine. And if somebody rang my bell or rang my telephone, I wouldn't even answer it.

Billie used to play in different clubs and different theaters. Anywhere around this territory she was, I was there. Wherever she was, I went: New Jersey or Connecticut. I didn't go further than that, like Washington or nothing. I read the story of her life. I tell you that poor girl went through hell trying to get where she got. Those fellas used to do her any kind of way. And when she died, I cried for days.

I got all of her old records. I got all kinds of albums of different people, not just Billie Holiday. Remember the 78s? I have some of them. I got Frank Sinatra, way back there. I got religious records. I got all kinds of albums. I don't bother with playing records anymore because I don't have the time to do it. I have my radio and my TV and there isn't enough time for them. Sometimes I sit up and listen to my old jazz on the radio and I listen to all my people, and I still have my bongos, but I'm finished with trying to bother with music. I stopped playing my saxophone and I'm not going to try to learn no piano now.

I got all them old records and when I get a little bit older, I might want to sit back and bring back the memories. I can listen to a piece on the radio now and so help me God, I can see myself perfectly in somebody's arms. I even feel their arms around me just because this piece is the piece that I used to dance by and is a piece that I love so much.

These days, if I'm walking in the street and I pass by a record shop, there's two people that stops me in my tracks if I happen to hear them: Billie Holiday and the Reverend Martin Luther King, Jr. I don't move until they finish what they're doing. The way that Dr. King talks, you just can't help but listen. Whatever he said, it made sense. And Billie, when she start singing her song . . .

I went in a hairdresser place the other day to see some friends, just to say hello. They was playing a piece on the radio by the Manhattans and I stopped right in my tracks on the street and I started dancing by myself. All I got to do is hear some music, I will stop in my tracks and start dancing in one minute. These guys, they were looking at me and they were saying, "Go ahead on, Momma." And I just carried on until the record was over. I'm not ashamed to dance. I'll stop anyplace if I hear some good music and I'll start dancing. I don't care who's looking at me.

I remember one year we went to Coney Island. It had to be in the forties because I was young then. Everybody was on the rides, or playing games. They had some music out there and do you know I went out and started dancing. You just give me some music and I'll really take the floor. Give me music, I'll dance on the table. Well, that day I had people just ganged around me. They just stopped playing the games. They just stopped riding, they stopped doing everything and ganged around me. And I did myself some dancing.

Anyplace I went, I used to take the dance floor every time. And I could almost dance by every beat that the band was playing. All I had to do was get me a guy who would do it. But I wanted him not to straight dance—I mean hold me, pull me back in, turn me around, and throw me back out. I wanted him to lead me out there and let me do what I wanted to do. If I was to say, "We get down," he'd get down. If he did everything I was doing, like to cut the fool—you know, have a good time— I loved that. He would probably have something that he would want to do and I'd see him do it and I'd want to do it too. If I find a guy like that, we'll take the floor. And everybody stand 'round, looking and clapping.

Now everybody's gone. All the good musicians are dead. All the good singers are dead. All them big people are gone. But that music ain't gonna never die. When somebody makes a record, that record lasts for years. Old music lasts forever. It's still out there. I can sit up all night and listen to old music. All this stuff they got today; something comes one week and the next week it's gone. These days, a record lasts for like two months. After about two months, nobody wants to hear it again.

Today funky is what the kids got in their music. That's what they say out there now, funk music. I don't know what they're thinking about. When I was growing up, we couldn't even say "funk." If you said, "She's funky," that meant she smelled. We used to go around the chair and smell whether the people that sat there was funky. Now funk for kids is music.

While I was still in school back home, I used to pick cotton. When time come for lunch, the man I was working for would bring his big old truck around every day at twelve o'clock. He had all kinds of food on it, everything you could name, like potato chips, baloney, sausage, cheese, cinnamon rolls. The people in the field used to go and get all that stuff but he wasn't giving the food away. He would write it on the book that you owed that and you owed the other.

I used to be very smart. I'd say to myself, "Now if I would take me an apple and a bun and a sandwich from home, I wouldn't have to buy all that stuff. So when time came to get my money, I'd have all of my money." I didn't buy anything from the man and when the time came to get paid off, I'd get more money than anybody, even the ones that picked more cotton than me. My name was not on his book and if you didn't buy anything, he couldn't put it there. That man got so mad at me, he didn't know what in the world to do.

I wanted to get out of the field so when I was about thirteen I asked a lady if she would talk with this man and ask him if I could leave picking cotton and come to work in the house for her. It's better if you got somebody on your side to talk for you. So the lady came down to the boss man of the field and said that she wanted me to work for her. I was so glad when she said she'd rather have me work for her in her house than in the field. Oh, I was in business then. I didn't have to pick cotton anymore. I got out of the cotton field because I couldn't pick cotton and work for her too.

Those people had a hardware store, and my job was to go and fix breakfast for the family every morning before I went to school. It was just like a little part-time job. I worked for them in the mornings before school, a few hours every day. I would come in and make a fire and make breakfast, and I'd make sure the table was set and see what else had to be done around there. Then I'd go to school; it wasn't like working out in the hot sun all day long. The lady didn't try to take me out of school. Sometimes she'd say, "Would you come back when you get out of school?" Most of the time I didn't come back because they ate their dinner at twelve o'clock and at twelve o'clock I was still in school. On Saturdays and Sundays there were more hours of work. I was paid very little for my work. I'm ashamed to tell how much so I'm not going to. It was very little but that was true for all of us back then.

When I worked for the hardware store people, I wanted me a bike, and I didn't want an old bike. I was poor but I just had to have a new bike. You were very popular with a bike in your kid days. It was like you were a little bit higher than the other kids. The hardware store sold bikes but the people that owned it wasn't going to just give me a brand-new one. I bought the bike and they charged me the full price. It cost me thirty-five dollars, and thirty-five dollars was money in those days. But I paid for it, little by little: fifty cents a week. I can't remember how long it took me but you know fifty cents grows pretty fast.

There was only one black girl in town that had a bike before I got one. She was the first colored kid of the girls with a bike and I was the second. The first boy that had a bicycle in town was the only child his mother had and it looked like they would give him everything. So there were three of us with bikes then.

I was working for them people in the hardware store when I left home and came up North to New Jersey. When I moved to New York after that, one way to get a job was to go up to the Bronx and stand in line on the street. White people would come along in their cars and choose which one of the girls they wanted to work for them. I said that I wasn't going to stand on no line and let somebody choose me. I wouldn't do that. If somebody picks you up on the street to take you to their house to work, you don't know whether that's going to be somebody that wants to harm you.

So I decided to go to an employment agency. I said I'm going to pay for my job. That way I can get a job and know that I'm gonna get paid for it and I'm gonna be safe. Because when they send you out, your name is in the book so you know where you're going and who you're working for. If anything happens to you, at least you know how to find out what happened. So every job I got, I paid for it. At that time, you had to pay about six dollars a job. When they sent you out and the lady accepted you, she would have to pay half and you would have to pay half: like a two-way street.

One time, two of us went out for the same job. The lady asked us what we could do. The other girl wanted the job so bad, she said, "I can do anything." I wanted the job too but when the lady got to me, I said, "I can do anything but I don't. Because if I could do anything, I can steal. I can lie." And you know that woman hired me. It's the way you have to talk.

I once worked in a factory for a week. You know how ads be in the paper that say, "Factory workers needed." So I went for that job. They were making decorations for hats—you know, these big hats they used to wear with flowers and feathers and everything. Some of the hats have a whole feather and some have a tiny little feather. If you wanted a hat with the little thing, you had to strip all that off the feather. Then somebody else would do with it what they had to do. We had a big table in the factory and everybody used to sit around it. I did what everybody else did to pull off the feathers; whatever the guy told me to do. But I didn't know that when you worked, he wanted you to hold your hands up in a certain way. I didn't know that you couldn't put your elbows on the table.

I worked in that factory Monday, Tuesday, and Wednesday. On Thursday, the man came to where I was sitting and knocked on the table. I said, "What do you want?" He said, "I don't want your elbows on the table. I want them off the table." I guess he figured that he's paying you but you're resting. I guess he thought, "Why should she be resting?" I was doing as much work as anybody else but the man didn't want it to be like that. It's like if you have a standing job, they don't want you to sit down. If you got a sit-down job, they don't want you to stand to do it. People used to be hard-hearted. I don't know how they could be like that.

When the man said that about the elbows, I told him, "I want my money right now because I'm going." He said, "Well, I can't give it to you right now. You have to wait until the week is up." I said, "Well, I'll wait until the week is up but I'm going now. When I come back Friday, just give me the days that I worked for this week." At the end of the week, I went back to the factory and I picked my money up. And from that day on, I've been doing private work in private homes.

In my jobs I started off with babies and went up to old people. I used to bring babies home from the hospital and stay with them until they'd get grown. In some jobs where I have been, I was the cook. Even when the children were around, I'd do the cooking and still take care of the kids.

The last family that I worked for, they had two kids. I worked for that family for many, many years. When I went to work there, I think I was about twenty-nine going on thirty and the mother was eight years older than me. When I started that job, the lady didn't have her little girl yet. I stayed with that family near Central Park from the time that little girl was born until she was eighteen years old. That was a long time to be with one family.

When I came, the little boy was about three. That was the cutest boy I've ever seen. And she dressed him so cute. He had the kind of color that if you get in the sun you could tan but not get red. He just had that kind of skin. And he had some black curls on his head. That was a pretty boy. Everybody thinks Kennedy's son is so pretty but I don't see anything handsome about Kennedy's son. He is just a guy. But when you know somebody who knows somebody—even when you're ugly—you're pretty. You understand what I mean. It's one of those things. When you got something, people build you up, you know. Kennedy's son is not that handsome. My boy would make him look like homemade goods. I almost told the lady, "Don't pay me no money. Just let me take care of that baby." I thought it but how could I say that? I thought, "Where do I get the money from, money that I needed to live?" So I didn't say it.

The lady had a job in a bank. I used to cook and clean and take care of the two kids. I did my work five days a week and went home every night. The family would go out of the city in the summer. July and August were the two months that I used to take off. I had the whole summer to myself. They paid me for it; I got my full salary. You give me the time off and I know what to do with it. I'd go visit people that I can't visit when I'm working. All I had to do is go down and maybe water the plants and see that the house was all right. I'd water them plants once a week; that was it. The house wouldn't get dirty. It might get a little dusty but what the hell am I gonna dust it for if nobody's there?

· · ·

I left that job on my own. My reasons for leaving started building up. The boy was in college and the little girl had just started college. The husband was dead and just the lady and I were there. I didn't want it like that. She didn't need me anymore. I tried to talk to her about it but she wouldn't listen to me. She was still working so she wanted me to stay too. I told her, "I don't want to work five days a week. I'm getting too old now, you know." (I wasn't old. I was in my late forties.) But I told her I was getting old and I needed to get some day's work.

After the boy got out of college, he got to be a restaurant manager. Some years ago, there was a fire in the hotel where he was living. There was a fire and he came down the steps and it met him. He got burned up in that fire and he died. (I don't see why he didn't go on the roof, but when it's your time . . .) He was a man when he got burned up. He wasn't no little boy. When his sister called me and told me, I just started hollering, "Oh, no. No. No. No. No."

My little girl calls me just to talk sometimes. She got married thirteen or more years ago. I was invited to the wedding. It was a beautiful affair. She just made forty-three herself back here in April. The parents are both gone now. She's the only one left in the family. She's the only one I hear from of all the kids I took care of. I guess the others done forgot. It was a long time ago, you know. Them people done grown up and some of them got their own children now.

It used to be that when I cooked for people, they would eat everything. But then they didn't eat everything because the doctors say you can't. This one's got to have this and that one's got to have that. I had to fix different meals for everybody but you don't get no raise. You still get the same money. I didn't think that's fair. So I said, "I'm not doing any more cooking." And I just stopped. Period. I said that from now on, I'm just going to get my day's work. When I was doing that day work, I wouldn't cook. I'd just do a little cleaning and come home.

When I had other jobs, I served quite a few dinner parties too. I didn't have to do the cooking; they would have caterers. But I would serve things and when they wanted me out there, they would tingle a little bell. I would bring out the food or stick it in the oven to reheat it or whatever.

And I would clean up afterward. I could clean up so fast it wasn't even funny. They would ask me did I want to use the dishwasher but it wasn't fast enough for me. I could do it much faster. I would get my water there and my Dawn. (You know Dawn is the best stuff for taking grease off.) I would wash the dishes and stack them up in there. I said to myself, "Why should I sit down when I know I have something to do. I know they gonna ring that bell when they need me. I sure can hear it because it ain't gonna be too far away. So I'll get my stuff together, rinse the dishes out and stand them up in there. Then when they ring, I'll go and serve them." When I came back in there, the dishes I got standing up done got dried. I made sure all that stuff was cleaned up before I left there. I went and crumbed the dining room—sometimes I'd use a sweeper, sometimes it would be a mop. I'd just make sure that no crumbs were under there when I left.

I made quite a bit of change messing around with those dinners. And they'd give me a pretty good tip too. I was doing everything so fast and I was paid by the hour. I guess they'd say, "She's saving me a couple of dollars." Now I don't know if the tip was for that reason. You don't ask people why they do things. If somebody did something nice for you, they did it. You don't ask no questions about it. And I'd do so good in there, if somebody else would have a party, they would tell that one. One time I was getting those jobs serving dinners two or three times a year.

That family I worked for, where I took care of the kids so long, I couldn't go to nobody else because I stayed with them too long. Sometimes way back there, I didn't have no real job. I had these little pieces of days that I was going around. It was kind of little hours. One time I went to two places in one day, just to make a decent little piece of money for that day. When I had the two jobs, I would go in the morning and get there about ten. They wanted four hours, so I'd get to the second job, let's say about two-thirty. That would be about a three-hour job. Sometimes I would have to catch a bus or a train to go to the other job. (It wasn't like I could just walk upstairs or go downstairs in the same building.)

All the time I been working, I never took one penny from the city for unemployment. If I got out of a job and I might stay out of it for a month or something, all my friends would say, "Why don't you go up and collect?" I never did that because I don't like to stand in anybody's line. I worked the whole time I've been in New York and the city got all the money because I have never collected one penny from them.

I always could get jobs because anything I did, I did it well. If I tell you I'm gonna do something, I do it. I don't play. If I can't do it well, I don't want to do it. Some people just want you to hurry it up. They say, "Give it a lick and a promise." Well, I can't lick and promise nothing. I really can't. If you tell me you want it done with a lick and a promise, I'd say do it yourself. You've got to give me the time to do it and to do it right because I don't want to half do it. Why should I do it if I can't do it right?

One thing about me is that I don't 'neg on anything. 'Neging means you don't do it. And I'm always on the job when I got to do it. I don't care what it's pushing. I don't care what it's pulling. I do my best to pull it or to push it. It's just something that's in me. And you don't have to be there to watch me. What I got to do, I do it. I don't class myself no straighter than anybody else. But if somebody give you a job to do and you don't want to do it, you should say so and don't do it. Don't go there and 'neg on the job. Don't do that and then want the money.

I've met quite a few people on the same job with me who don't feel that way. If I'm doing something, they don't want me to do it. They try to talk me out of it. They say, "Oh, why are you doing all of that?" They think I'm trying to butter up the boss but that's not the point. He gave me a job to do and I'm gonna do it. I would never tell on them but I just don't want to work with them. Most of the time they make you do all the work. Especially if you were there first. The people that hired you are gonna look to you like you should've seen that the job was done right. I've done lots of people's work because I didn't want the boss to say, "Two people are in here and this place look like this." In some places, they had a laundress, they had a cook, and they had somebody to take care of the kids. Now in them kind of places, I didn't stay too long. Maybe that's why I'm still alive today, because I've always been working by myself.

And I'm not going to recommend nobody to work. People used to ask me all the time in places where I was working if I knew somebody but I won't tell them. How do I know what them people will do? I don't live with them people. They are not my sister or my brother. I don't know what they'll do. If they did something wrong, it would get back to Freddie Mae. The people will say, "Well, Freddie Mae knew her." So if you ask me to recommend somebody, I'm gonna tell you that I don't know anybody.

I never took much time off from work. In my younger days, I used to have a very bad period every month. I had a very bad time. The lady I worked for would give me quite a few days off because she knew I was very sick with it. And I always did tell her that I would make the time up some kind of way.

I'd be angry, very angry, when I'd be sick and somebody bothered me at home. I'll tell them in the beginning, "If I call and say that I'm feeling bad and I can't make it, please believe me." All the people I worked for believed me because they knew that if I have something to do, I'm gonna do it. If I can't do it, I'm gonna let you know that I can't do it today. And ain't no use to try to talk me into it, because if I can't do it today, I'm not going to do it today. And if I call you and tell you that I'm sick, I don't want you calling me every day to find out how I'm feeling. I want you to forget about me, because when you call I'm thinking you're calling to find out when I'm coming back to work. When I'm ready—which is when I'm feeling well—I'm coming back. You don't have to worry about me.

I'll never forget the 17th of March one year in the late 1950s. We had snow so bad until you couldn't go out even with boots on. I called the lady I was working for and told her I wasn't coming to work. She said, "Maybe about eleven o'clock or something, you might be here." I said, "I'm not coming. I was out there with boots on and you couldn't make it." She said the weather might change and the snow might go down or whatever. I said, "I'm not coming today. Maybe tomorrow. But today, I'm not coming."

When I was working for another lady and the weather was bad, she would call me up and say, "Don't come today because the weather is too bad." I'd say to her, "If the subway is running I'm coming, because there's gonna be days that I really cannot come. I want you to think about that." I'd tell her, "I got boots. I got a raincoat. I got a hat. I got an umbrella. I'm not sick. I'm coming." I tell all of them, "I don't care if there's rain, sunshine, hot, or cold, I will be there unless it's really too bad and the trains or buses done stopped." (You know I can't do anything about that, 'cause I'm not going to walk from Harlem to the job.)

A boss is supposed to be the boss. And I wouldn't want to work for a boss that lets you come in and say anything you want to them. Any boss that lets you talk back to them, they shouldn't be a boss. That's the way I feel about it. I see some girls and they say certain things on the job. I'm not going to do it; I would never talk back to a boss. You can call me an underdog or any kind of dog you want but I'm not going to fuss with my boss. I'm very honest. I try to be fair with people. I might answer him back and tell him exactly how I feel. I have to tell him like it is but to fuss with him like word for word, word for word, you don't do that. I couldn't do any arguing or cursing. If your boss lets you do that, he's no boss.

Now that don't mean I'm gonna let somebody put my head on the floor. I don't have to take no kind of shit if I don't want to. I always had only me to take care of. I never had any children that I had to say that I have to do something to take care of my children. Don't get me wrong. I'm gonna be nice. I'm gonna do what you ask me to do if I can do it. I'm not going to do anything to make you mad at me if I can help it. But you just ain't gonna put your foot on me.

I think you should give your boss respect and I believe that he'll give it back to you. In any job that I have, if a man is my boss I want to know his name when I get there. If I ask his name and he tells me "Jim," I say, "I want to know Jim What." He's gonna give me his whole name and I'm gonna call him his last name. With me, it's always going to be Mr. So-and-so and Mrs. So-and-so. That way, you and I can stand on an equal basis. You treat me like I'm your worker and I treat you like you're my boss.

If he tell me Jim Green, that man's name is gonna be Mr. Green as far as I'm concerned. If I call him Jim and he wants to come and pinch me, then he thinks that I'm going to turn around and laugh like it's okay. But if I work for him, he's not going to do that to me. I won't have him pulling and pinching on me and then think that I'm going to laugh. If he does that, I'll turn around and say, "Mr. Green." And I'll hit him. I don't want him to tell me to call him this or call him that and then if his friends are around and I happen to call him that name, he's gonna whisper to me, "Call me So-and-so-and-so." Now that makes me mad because I been calling you So-and-so all the time.

I have had the problem of a man bothering me on the job and I tried to stop it right away. (People don't know nothing that happens behind closed doors.) If there was a man who gave me any trouble where I was working, I'd say, "I'm not going to have all that pinching and you saying, 'Oh, I'm just teasing.' I don't like it like that. You just forget the whole thing because I'm not gonna work for you and let you pinch and tease me." I'd say, "Now you're not gonna tease me if I'm working for you. If you want to tease me, then don't have me working for you. You just come and be my man." I'd say, "I'm not coming into your home and work for you if I got to be worrying about when I bend over or whatever I do 'cause I'm scared of you." That's what I told them. I'm right up front. I tell them exactly how it is. You can tell it nice enough so that somebody won't think you're being rude. I hate being rude. I'm not really a rude person but I will tell you exactly how I think.

I always liked to take care of women because one time I was taking care of an old man and it was no good. He was in his eighties and he'd grab me. (A man don't ever think he gets too old for that. I don't care how old he is; it's still in his mind.) And quite naturally I'd say, "Don't you do that now. That's not nice." The man had a wife but she was out working and I was there alone with him. And I'd be scared to death because I didn't know what he was going to do. Even if he had caught me, I wouldn't have hit him. I would never hurt him, you know. He was sick. So I said, "I'm gonna wash your back and then I'm gonna give you the washrag and let you wash all the private parts yourself." And I said to myself, "Oh, Lordy. If I ever get away from this, I'm not gonna deal with them men. From now on, it's gonna be women."

Nothing beats being your own boss. I never wanted to be under somebody's thumb. I can't let somebody control me. I don't want to get myself so deep in anything that if I wanted to leave, I couldn't leave there. (That's why I believe I didn't try my best to get a bigger job.) I wouldn't say that I wouldn't do something if my boss would ask me to do it and I knew it was in reason. I would do that because she's paying me. If it's something that I think I shouldn't be doing and you ask me to do it, I might do it. The only way I would do it is that I cared a whole lot for you. But if I didn't care all that much for you, I would turn you down.

Anybody that I accepted a job from and I stayed, that meant I liked them. (If you don't want to be there, you can quit anytime you wanted. There's not something that somebody can hold on to you.) I loved my people 'cause if I didn't love them I wouldn't want to be around them. You could never get me away from my person. Nobody could take me away from them unless they made me mad, or they fired me. Even if you paid me more money to go somewhere else, you couldn't get me away from there unless I wanted to come from there. I think the others could be jealous how I treated those people. Because I was really, really good to them; I treated them with so much respect and I did my job. You know sometimes you can treat the person with respect and don't do your job. Sometimes you don't have both. But I did. I treated them good and I did my work.

I hated working for friends or family. Like if I was working for you and you had a sister or a mother and you said to me, "Freddie, do you think you could help my sister or my mother?" And I might go and work for your sister or your mother, or whoever it is. Then let's say I might do something for you that you don't even ask me to do. I'll do it because I think it's gonna make you happy. (There are things I will just do on my own to please you.) Like you might have a gold trim around your fireplace screen and it done got tarnished. So after I get through with my work, I'm gonna shine that up. And when you come back, it's gonna hit you right in the eye. You might say to me, "Oh, Freddie, that looks so nice. I'm going to give you a little something extra."

Then your sister comes and she gonna want me to do that for her. She might tell me, "Oh, you cleaned her fire screen." But you didn't ask me to do it. I did that on my own. So why somebody got to ask me to do it when I did it for you on my own? I don't want to do the same thing for everybody. The lady I was working for who asked if I could help her sister, she said, "Oh, Freddie Mae. You don't have to do it long as you stay with me and do it for me." And I said, "I will because I'm not going to work for them. If I'm working for you, don't try to introduce me to anybody, because I'm not going."

You had to make adjustments on the job. I worked for people and did the things they wanted me to do and I got paid. I never got fired on the job. If I left, I quit on my own. Nobody ever fired me. But I always tried to leave in a way that left room for talk. Why are you gonna leave mad? When we've been together for so long, I don't want to leave on the job that we can't say hello to each other. You can never tell when you might meet again.

I have worked for people who have to do something to make you halfway angry. People will do that. Sometimes I used to get so mad at work, I'd go in another room: When I get upset, I walk away. I won't talk to the people and that will hurt them much worse than if you hit somebody. If there's somebody who wants to talk to you and you don't talk, that bothers them. I won't talk if I get angry. I just leave the room and I'll go in the kitchen. If I was still angry when I got home, I'd either talk to myself or talk to my friends.

One day, I was talking on the telephone in this person's house. I was saying to my friend, "I'm gonna tell her off. You know where I'm coming from. I'm gonna tell her off." Then the door opened and there she was. I know she heard me but she acted like she didn't. She didn't say anything. I guess she didn't want to embarrass me and I didn't want to embarrass her. But she heard what I said.

Another time, I got so mad at the same lady till I was dripping blood. (Not really, that's just a phrase that I'm saying.) I was so angry and upset, I didn't sleep all night long. One mind tell me to don't go back there. One mind say, "Tell her off." I just carried on about what I was gonna say when I walked in there the next morning.

The next day I was so huffed up that the train wasn't going fast enough for me. I was almost driving it myself, trying to hurry and get there. When I got there and put the key in the door, I got ready to start telling her off but nobody was in the house. I have never been so disappointed in my life. I just started hollering and crying. I just cried like a baby. I wished she had walked in then. She would've wanted to know what I'm crying about. I cried and cried and when I got that cry out, so help me God, it was like a white cloud came over me. The black cloud was gone. You know I didn't think about it anymore. I didn't even think about it. When she got there, it was all gone.

I think God fixed it so that nobody was in that house when I got there. The kids were gone to school; she was gone. That Guy Upstairs, He helps us. We don't know it but He is there to help us. I was getting ready to say, "You know what, you so-and-so-and-so." It's a funny thing about people. If you don't tell your boss that you're upset, then tomorrow they done forgot about you and that you got upset last night. That lady acted like everything was the same.

I know many old people you work for will do something to make you halfway angry, but I'm a calm person. Most of the time, I stay cool. I try to keep things calm. I say, "Yes, ma'am." I say, "Okay." But sometimes that ain't enough for them, you know what I mean? They'll keep badgering, badgering, badgering you in some kind of way to get you upset. They'll do anything to get you upset. When they provoke you and you get very angry, it lifts them up because they done got you mad. Because they know that if they can upset somebody, they are still alive. Once they get you upset, they are living. You can almost see it in their face. They have a look that says, "I got her." Now they can lay back and rock and go to sleep.

I have worked for people that people say they couldn't work for. There's people that have a job to do and every time they get somebody, they didn't stay. The girls that left, they told me, "Oh, I can't work for her. You're not gonna be able to work for her." And I would go there and I'd stay for years. I think it's the way you carry yourself. Maybe it's because I treat you like I would like you to treat me. If you treat me cruel, I'll turn around and give you a smile. I try to be kind if I can: Kindness rubs off on different people. I'll look at you and smile in a minute because I laugh all the time. And it's gonna hurt you. Don't say it won't, because it's gonna hurt you. And you'll want to say, "Oh, I should apologize, I hurt her feelings . . ."

The most difficult person I ever worked for was just too fast on the draw. Like one day, I just walked in the door, put on my working clothes, went in the kitchen and got a bucket because I was going to clean the bathroom first. I went in the bathroom but I came right back because I forgot something in the kitchen. And the lady said, "You finished the bathroom?" I said, "I just got here. I just went from the kitchen to the bathroom. I forgot something and came out." I said, "How fast can I clean the bathroom? I'm not Speedy Gonzalez." She said, "Oh, I'm sorry. I just didn't know."

Another thing happened with her. She was a real-estate lady and I was working first for this other lady that was the boss of the real-estate place. But something went wrong and I told the other lady I was quitting. When the real-estate boss told this lady that I had quit her, she told her boss that she could get me to come back. She told me, "Freddie Mae, why don't you go back to her? You know you can go back." Now nobody can get me to do anything if I don't want to do it. I don't care what you do or how you do it. If I don't want to do it, you can't get me to do it. Now the lady was very, very smart but I think she was trying to do too much. I said to her, "I don't appreciate what you did. Please don't do it again because if you do, I'm not going to stay with you. I'm going to leave. I won't have you doing me like that."

There was one lady I worked for who was one of the nicest people that you could ever lay eyes on. The only thing I disliked about her was that she always grabbed me by the coat when I walked in. She'd say, "Oh, that's a nice coat you got on." I think it's all right to say I got on a nice coat but don't grab me. I kind of disliked her for that but outside of that, I liked her. I used to do anything for her. I put in all the lightbulbs rather than call the maintenance men in her building. You know the maintenance men have their hand out for you to give them something just to come and put in a lightbulb. So I saved her money because I did the little things for her that the maintenance men would do.

This lady was an old woman and she happened to meet a man. He was old too, and they got together; he started staying there and everything. All of a sudden, you could feel the difference in how she was treating me. She'd say, "You have to put a lightbulb up in the kitchen." I said to myself, "Now if she had asked me the right way like we been talking before, it would've been all right." But the way she put it, it pissed me completely off. When he started staying there, I said to myself, "He's a man. I ain't supposed to put up no more lightbulbs." I said to her, "I'm not going to put it up." She said, "What? You're not going to put it up?" I said, "That's what I said." I told her, "I'm not gonna put any more lightbulbs up now. You got a guy. He can get up there and put the lightbulb in. I did it for you because otherwise you would have to send down for the main-

tenance men. I did it for you but I'm not gonna do it for him."
So I quit the job. She got somebody else to come in there and
work for her.

After I quit her, I was still working in the same building
for another lady down the hall. One day that lady said to me,
"Freddie Mae, do you know the girl that works for So-and-so?"
I said, "No, I don't know her." Then she told me that the girl
done took all the old woman's silver. Now all the time I was
there working, I'm shining up and shining up her silver and
she still has it. Then somebody walks in there and it's gone.

When I hear things like that, it bothers me so much. Some
people got sticky fingers. They just can't stand to be around
things. It bothers them to be around something and they don't
take it. Like you could have a good job and mess it up because
you took ten dollars. Some people give up good jobs for ten
dollars, five dollars, even two dollars. I don't want the darn
money. I'd rather keep my job any day.

Most jobs I stayed with two or three years. But I don't
think I stayed with anybody longer than I stayed with Miss
Hansen. I stayed with her almost twenty years. You know how
some people might say that they don't like white people but I
loved that woman as if she was my mother. If she had been my
mother, I don't think that she could've been more to me. I
treated her with the kind of respect that I would want anybody
to have for my mother.

I just figure that if you got a job to do, you got a job to do
and loving can go along with any job. Miss Hansen said I
spoiled her and I told her that I didn't care. I said, "Anybody
that I love and I care for, I am going to be as nice as I can to
them." Loving can go along with any job. You don't have to
pay for that. Miss Hansen got me back into cooking. And I
used to wash her windows all the time when I wouldn't wash
nobody else's. Miss Hansen was ninety-one when she died. She
was out of the city in a nursing home then.

She had beautiful skin. Some people get old and their skin stays nice, but there's some people her age, so help me God, you'd swear that they were a hundred and fifty. She used to say that she wasn't a good-looking woman. But I'd say to her, "Miss Hansen, some people your age is all skootched up. Some people get those lines." But she wasn't; she kept a beautiful nice skin like she wasn't too old. Some people, you know, just keep a nice face. I didn't say she was pretty. I said she was a good-looking lady, but not pretty. She didn't believe it when I told her that. I said, "Okay, if you don't believe it, forget about it."

I started working for her when she got out of the hospital. She was operated on for her stomach and she needed somebody to work for her. At the time, I was working for a friend of her friend. So the lady asked me would I come and talk with Miss Hansen. Me and Miss Hansen clicked just like that. I liked her. There was just something about her. I said, "I really hope that we'll get along." And we did. We just got along so well. We would speak about it every once in a while. All through the years we would speak about it. I stayed with her until she left me.

I cared for the people on the jobs I worked for. There was only one I didn't like. I worked for her awhile, then I left. She knew Miss Hansen. She told her, "You just wait until she be ready to leave you." When Miss Hansen told me that, I bust out in a big old laugh. I said, "Miss Hansen, I'm gonna call her bluff. I'm gonna stay with you until you leave me because I'm not gonna let her say 'I told you so.'" I kept Miss Hansen laughing, I swear to God.

That lady was my baby. I bet she just rolls over in heaven because I talk about her all the time. It's gonna be a long time before I get up there myself. When I told Miss Hansen that I love her but I don't love her *that much,* it made her laugh. She always did tell me, "You're the cause of me living longer 'cause you always got something to make me laugh about."

While Miss Hansen was still living at home, I wished that she would let me get her out of the house more. But she was ashamed to be going around like with a walker or a cane or in a wheelchair. I get around pretty good for my age but if I had to walk with two canes, I wouldn't be ashamed because at least I'd be walking. Some people want none of that; they have to sit. But other people, if you tell them they had to walk on two or three sticks, they would do it. Miss Hansen was ashamed to do that. I don't know why. I used to beg her, "Let's walk." But I could only get her to walk in the hallway outside her apartment. And sometimes she'd be so tired. I used to tell her, "If you don't use them, baby, you're going to lose them." And that is the truth. Anything you've got, if you don't use it, you're going to get so you can't and you're gonna do nothing but quit. So I said, "Miss Hansen, you gotta get up and walk. If you don't, your legs are not gonna hold up for you." And they didn't.

After a while, somebody was there with her every day. If I wasn't there, one of the girls who worked for her was there. When I wasn't there, Miss Hansen was trying to carry her dinner from the kitchen in her arm with her cane and she was falling and breaking things. So I made a nice little basket for her with a handle. It was big enough to set her little plate down in there, her glass of whatever she gonna drink—a cup of tea or whatever—and a little dessert. Then she got her stick. She went to the kitchen and got her basket and that worked out.

Miss Hansen wouldn't have broken that hip if she had've listened to me. I told her over and over, "Don't take anything in your hand that's heavy." One day I came in and looked in the bed. She wasn't there. I saw a chair was turned over and a box was turned over. I was just getting ready to jump around to the bathroom. Then I looked and she was laying down on the floor behind the bed. She pulled the sheet up and had the spread over her while she was laying down there.

Miss Hansen had picked up a box of papers that she had on the shelf in that little hallway and she had tried to take it into the bedroom. She must've lost her balance. She probably dropped the box or whatever, because the box was on the floor. I don't know if she fell that night or if she fell that morning. I don't know when she fell and she couldn't tell me. When she broke her hip, they had to put her in a nursing home.

Miss Hansen kept a lot of cash around her house so I was very scared when I was working there. Nobody knew about it but me. Every time I'd go to the bank for her, I'd get a thousand dollars. When time come to go back to the bank and get another thousand, she'd still have quite a bit left. I was the only other one who knew where it was. I was scared about her having all that money around. You don't know whose money it is. (There ain't nothing on it but them presidents.) I had the money in her file cabinet but I had it in a place that only she and I knew where it was. They would have to look their heads off to find it.

I'd always make sure she'd get enough out just to have it in a drawer in case one of the girls who worked for her had to go and get some of it to pay for something. I was scared that one day she might miss and let them girls know where the money is at.

When she left that place to go to the nursing home, there was about four thousand dollars in the house. There was this lady who watched out for Miss Hansen. I told her about the money. I told her that Miss Hansen always let me get money from the bank and I would always put it in a certain place. I said to her, "Here it is." And I gave her every penny of it. She told me, "Freddie Mae, you keep it." She said, "Pay yourself each week because you know you still got to live regardless of what happens." (I had told her exactly what Miss Hansen paid me.) She was really nice. That lady was beautiful. She really did treat me nice. She said, "Pay yourself till it's all gone." And she told me to pay the train and the taxi fare up there to the nursing home. She knew I was going to be honest. I used that money to go and visit Miss Hansen in the nursing home until it all went. It lasted a long time because I didn't touch it for any other thing. Everything worked out all right.

I got unhappy when I was up there in the nursing home where Miss Hansen was. One lady there, who was in Miss Hansen's room, used to bother me. She used to ask me to leave Miss Hansen and go someplace with her. I said, "No, honey, I can't. I'm here with Miss Hansen." The nurses said the lady would get very upset when I came because she thought I was her guest. When I'd go in the dining room with Miss Hansen, the lady would be someplace looking and laughing because she just think that I came there to see her. They had to restrain her because she wanted to be with me.

I hated for her to feel bad, but I was only there for two and a half hours and I wanted Miss Hansen to have every bit of it. I wanted her to have all of me. Even if she was asleep, I wanted to be right there. The other lady probably didn't have many visitors and that's so hard. I wish that I sort of could love both of them, you understand what I mean? But I couldn't because I had to give Miss Hansen my time.

When Miss Hansen was in the nursing home, she didn't want to be fed. She didn't want nobody to put that spoon up to her mouth. She said, "Freddie Mae, I do not want nobody to feed me." When they tried to feed her, she'd bite down on the fork. They didn't want her to break her teeth out so they would let her try to feed herself in the dining room. But she wouldn't be able to eat fast enough. Then if they stayed with her longer, she'd get uninterested in the food and didn't want no parts of it. When I was there, I put the food on the fork and let her know she could put it up into her mouth if she wanted to. The nurses said to me, "If you were here every day, she might come out of it. She might gain some of her weight back." But I could only go up there once a week.

Miss Hansen was tired, and she just wanted to leave this world. She could walk after she broke her hip but she wouldn't because she didn't have nobody who could take the time for her. The nursing home she was in was a beautiful place but I think she figured that she just wasn't being treated right. She was so used to somebody loving her and caring for her. Miss Hansen didn't have no private nurses. Up there in the nursing home, people don't have time for you. They had to do what they had to do. They would say, "When we get there, we get there."

I took good care of Miss Hansen. I don't think she could've had her own daughter who could've cared any more.

If Miss Hansen is up there looking down, I know she'd say, "You took good care of me, Freddie Mae. Yes, you did." There's tears in my eyes, but I'm not gonna cry 'cause I don't cry. But I think about her sometimes. And I dream about her pretty often. But in my dream, she won't come and tell me the Lotto numbers. Why don't she come and do that for me? She know I ain't making no money. Even if she gave me the wrong number, I would still love her.

Girls are doing everything now, you know—all kinds of jobs. I see girls doing construction work on the street. They got that machine that digs up the street and puts the dirt in the trucks. Every time I see them, I try to have a conversation with them. They laugh and talk to me. I say, "Right on. Right on, girl." I tell them, "You go ahead and make that money." There's a little man working there, he says something about it. I say to him, "You leave it alone. These girls gonna do you all in. They gonna make that money too."

In my time, we couldn't do that. They didn't want to be bothered with us. They had us thinking that if we did something like a boy, we weren't a girl anymore. We had to be girls all the time. They always wanted us to be feminine and everything. So I told the girls doing construction work that I wish I was up there now where I could make some of it myself, 'cause I sure would do it if I could.

"Go girl," I tell them, "you go ahead and make that money for yourself."

CHILDREN

Ihave brought up quite a few white people's kids in my time—over maybe twenty different kids—and I think I did a pretty good job with some of them.

There's three levels in a child before they're grown and I know every one of them. When they were little, I treated them as little. I tried to do the best I could to keep them happy. (What a kid needs is happiness.) When they get up a little bigger, when they want to run a little bit faster, that's another level. Then when they get a little up there, the girls are peeking around the boys, and that's the third level. Each level of the child needs something different.

When I took care of a baby that's getting to be nine or ten months old, I would tell the mother when she was going out, "Kiss him and say goodbye. And when you walk out the door, you keep right on going whether he cry or not. Keep right on going. If you come back, you gonna make my job hard." The mothers listened to me. I'm talking the truth so they can't get mad and say I'm being fresh. I told them, "If you come back, they gonna cry every day." That's the way with them kids. But if they see you not coming back, they think, "What the hell. She's not coming back so why should I cry and hurt myself and wet my eyes up?"

When I was taking care of kids, I always made them share.

If I gave one an apple, I made sure that the other one got one too. I don't care what it is, if there's a brother and a sister or two sisters or two brothers, whatever, you've got to share. I'd say, "If you're not going to give her any, I'm not going to give it to you." That's how it was in my family, and that's how kids should be.

You keep teaching them. They may not want to do it but after a while, they say, "That old son-of-a-gun, she ain't gonna let us get by with this here jive. We may as well go ahead and do it." Then after they grow up, they'll want to share with their brother and sister.

I brought my kids up not to be looking for something all the time. If Grandmother came and she brought something, that's fine. And if she didn't bring anything, that's fine too. (Maybe Grandma didn't have a chance to go to the store.) If Grandma brings something every time but one day she isn't able to bring it, then the kids would say, "Oh, it's only Grandma." I told them, "If Grandma brings you something, go and kiss her. If she didn't bring you anything, go and kiss her." I wanted my kids to know that they couldn't have their way on everything.

When I'd take the children to the park, some of the nurses (in that time, we were calling each other nurses) would be hollering and whooping at the kids, cursing them and screaming. Now, I'm not gonna have that. I don't care how much I love the kids, they're not going to curse me, because I'm not going to curse at them. Kids will not curse you out if you don't curse them out.

I say the best thing for you to do is call that kid over and talk to him. If you go out there and say, "Come right in here because I'm gonna do so-and-so-and-so to you," if you say that, you done embarrass the kid before his friends. And the other kids say, "Your momma is a so-and-so." Now the next time she come out there and start that again, you know the kid is gonna say something that's gonna really hurt her.

Because when you embarrass a kid before his friends, that's when he says things to you that he wouldn't ordinarily say. I think you should call him over and say, "Now you know that I told you to don't do so-and-so-and-so." If you don't let nobody hear it but him, he's not going to talk back to you. Let's say there's a group of kids out playing and having a good time. Now if you said to a kid before you left home, "You got to do this, you got to do that, you got to do the other . . . ," and when you come back and see he didn't do what you told him to do, you're going to the door and you're going to holler at him where his friends can hear. You're gonna say, "I told you to make up that bed! I told you to do so-and-so-and-so!"

Then that kid will rebel. He gonna turn around and say, "Oh, will you shut up!" or something and it can be his mother too. Embarrassment causes you to do things that you wouldn't ordinarily do. That kid will turn around and tell you the same thing that you said whether you're his mother or not because you made him ashamed. You get him away from his friends so his friends don't hear you, and you say whatever you need to say to him; then you won't have any trouble. Some people make kids talk back to them because they don't treat them like a kid. You shouldn't embarrass a person.

I never screamed at the kids. If I did want to say something, I'd say it quietly. If you want the boy to do something, you call him over and you talk to him and not to his friends. If they start coming too, you tell them to go ahead on. You say to them, "Go ahead and play." You want to talk to your child and tell him what you got to tell him.

I didn't have to beat them kids. When I'd take them to the park, I'd sit up and say, "Do anything you want but let me see you. Just don't get out of my sight." (Because in the park with them rocks and things like that, somebody can be lurking behind and grab one of them kids and pull them out.) The kids would play on the rocks. They would play on the monkey bars. I could sit right in my seat and let them play as much as they want to as long as they didn't hurt themselves. I'd say to the girl, "Go and play with your dolly." I'd say to the boy, "Go and dig," because the boy loved to dig. I didn't care who I was talking to in the park, I kept my eye on those kids.

The girl would swing her dolly. The boy was digging out. I told the little girl, "I know the swings are out here for you to swing." I said, "If you want to swing your dolly in there until the other kids come, then I'll swing you with the other kids. But I'm not gonna swing you now, and then when the other kids come, swing you again." She took her little dolly and she'd swing it. I'd sit there and look at her swinging. Then, when all the kids start coming in the park, she'd come and get me and I'd swing her along with the other kids.

I said to her brother, "If you want to dig or climb the monkey bars or whatever you want, you do it until your little friends come. Then I'll put you in there on the swings and let you swing." I said, "I'm not gonna do it all the time because I'm not out here to swing you all day long." And I didn't have no problem with him, either.

Then when time came to go because I got to cook dinner, all I had to do was stand up and stretch and them kids came right to me. They'd come right along with me. I didn't have to holler. The other nursemaids would want to know how I done that. I said, "It's the way you raise them, that's all. You don't go there, hollering and screaming and yelling at them. You treat them as human beings and they treat you as one."

Those kids respected me. They weren't calling me all kinds of things and cursing me in the street. I didn't have one white kid that could walk up to me and say they gonna spit on me. And I have seen it in the park with the other girls that was out there taking care of kids. Those kids come and kick them and do all like that. I raised them kids up from babies. Of all the children I brought up in my life, I never had one say a curse word to me. Not one has gotten out there and said something bad to me. My children loved me because of the way I treated them.

There was only one little boy who said he was gonna kick me. I said, "Yeah, you see that leg you got there, I'm gonna break it." If you tell them you gonna break their leg when their mother is out, then you better tell them you are gonna break their leg when their mother is in there. That way the kid knows you mean it. Of course, you're not gonna break his leg, but the kid thinks you're gonna do it. He thinks, "Oh, she didn't get scared of my momma. She said it right in front of my momma, so she'll probably do it." The mother knew I was gonna teach that kid for picking his leg up to say he was gonna kick me and I ain't never had no more trouble with that kid.

I did the same thing when Momma was there that I did when Momma wasn't there. The kids knew I didn't wait until Momma was around to be so friendly and then when Momma is not around, I'd slap them. You be mean to the kids when the mother is not there. Then when the mother comes, you go "kootchie, kootchie, koo" to the kids. That same way I treat them when the mother's not there is the way I treat them when the mother is there. That's the way you gotta raise them kids. Let's say you're teaching them to don't do this when Momma is not here but when Momma is here, you let them do it just to please Momma, or whatever it is. The kids get all confused. The best way is to do the same thing at all times.

All you got to do is love the kids. I loved all my kids that I took care of. The parents—if they were still alive—could say, "Oh, that girl was good to my kids." They knew if I said something, I meant what I said. One night the mother was on the telephone and me and the kids had something going, not bad stuff—nothing like that—but I probably said something too loud. The other lady on the phone heard it and she said, "Who is that yelling?" My boss said, "Oh, that's Freddie Mae and the kids." And the friend said, "Oh, you let her yell like that in your residence?" My boss caught the lady right then. She said to her, "Don't say nothing. What Freddie is doing, that's what Freddie is doing. I don't have anything to do with that." 'Cause she knew I was good to her kids.

Sometimes the kids would rather see me than their mother. But I always did teach them, "Unh. Unh. Unh. That's your mother. I am your nurse and I'm gonna do the best I can for you but that's your mother." I said, "You're not gonna tell me that you're not gonna do what Momma say do. You will do what Momma say you do."

I used to live on the east side of Park Avenue. People get confused when you say you live on Park Avenue. The first thing they figure is you're down there with the big shots. I was on Park Avenue but not downtown Park Avenue. I was up higher. I was on 129th Street.

For all the little children around there, I was like a big teddy bear. Years ago, I'd come home from work and there'd be a truck out there with a little Ferris wheel on it. When I'd see those kids, I would hand the guy with the truck a ten-dollar bill and tell him to ride the kids until the money go. I said to him, "When it go, you leave it alone." And that ten dollars would've rode all of them, all of them; some of them twice. I say, "Have your hand open for people. Don't close it. Especially for children."

I knew some of them kids and some of them I didn't know. But if I give one I know a ride and don't give a ride to the one that I don't know, it would put me right back when I was a young girl and when people used to do that to me. Like if you bring the other kids a gift or something and I'm standing there and you don't give me anything. That never got out of my heart. I don't mean I hate anybody or dislike anybody because people have to do what they have to do. If that's what they want to do, that's their business. But for me myself, if I don't have any money for all the kids, I'm not going to give it to any of them.

The parents were wondering, "How come you do that? Ain't none of them kids yours." I said, "It doesn't make any difference." They say the way to a man's heart is through his stomach. Well, a way to a mother's heart is through her kids. If you love her kids, you can't do much wrong.

There were lots of kids on my block and I loved them all. They could be doing something bad—when I say bad, they could be fighting or doing something else—but if they saw me, they'd say, "Miss Freddie Mae is coming." And they'd stop it. I never scolded them; I loved them and they had respect for me.

About thirty years ago, when I was getting ready to move away from Park Avenue, I decided I wanted to do something for the kids for them to remember me by. So I gave a big going-away party and I asked the kids ages seven to ten that lived on the block to come. (They couldn't come if they were under seven because I didn't want them crying.) I told the kids, "You tell your mothers that I'm giving a party and I want you to come but you got to be dressed up."

One of the girls, she was kind of fresh. She told all the other kids, "I'm not going." She just wanted to mess up their minds to see whether they were gonna say, no, they weren't coming either. When they told me that she was not coming, I said, "Okay. That will be one less, that's all." And do you know, that girl was the first one at the door!

When the time came for the party, the kids came running, running down the hallway, like something was behind them. They were all dressed up: little shined shoes; little socks; the girls had their hair curled up and the boys, you could see that their hair had been washed and cleaned. Every one of those kids I invited came.

I had two big old pound cakes. I had ice cream. I had soda.

I had potato chips and peanuts. I made lemonade. I served ice cream. I served punch. We had candy. We had bobbing for apples in the tub. And I had music for them. At that time, people were playing records, not tapes. I put on all my 45s and played dance music for them.

Then, late in the afternoon, one little girl came up and whispered in my ear, "Miss Freddie Mae, can the girls ask the boys for a dance?" I said, "Girl, you have a good idea there." Oh, could those little kids get down, they really danced. When they got ready to leave, I had little bags for them to take home, with candy and a stick of gum inside. At that time, things weren't quite as high as they are now but I didn't care what it cost. Just to know that I made those kids happy when I was getting ready to move out of the neighborhood.

Sometimes those same kids meet me in the street and they always say, "Miss Freddie Mae, we'll never forget you because you were really good to us when we was coming up." And it just makes me feel so good. They have their own kids now. Some of them are even grandmothers. And maybe they're just thinking, "There ain't nothing like Miss Freddie Mae."

I guess they haven't ever forgotten this face. You don't see too many faces that look like mine. Sometime I'll be in the train and those kids in the train just be looking at me. They just be looking. I ask myself, "Do you reckon you look all right? Do you think there's something on your face? Something might be on your nose." I told my doctor one time about the little kids looking at me. I was thinking he might tell me why it happens. He said, "Little kids are like a dog. A dog knows right away whether you like him or not."

You know ordinary kids would come and talk to me about things that maybe they wouldn't talk to their mothers about because I will listen. The kids talk to me about anything: sex, boyfriends, girlfriends, whatever. I don't cut them off but I would prefer them not to be telling me. I don't like for them to do that, 'cause if the mother finds out, she might think I'm taking over her kid. But I will sit back and listen to them so they figure that they have somebody that they can talk to. Mostly I listen to see what they got to say. If there's something that I have to give advice on, I give it to them. If not, I just listen because kids have things to say and they want you to listen to them.

I guess kids know that I like them. I should've had me about five: two girls and three boys, that would have been beautiful. I like boys better than I like girls but I won't let them know it. I have been around both of them but I don't know why I like the boy children much better. A little boy, you brush his hair, wash his face, put a little pair of dungarees on him or a little pair of pants, and you're out the door. Little girls, you have to fuss over them, comb their hair and so on. But you try to treat all of the kids the same.

I don't care how many you got, one of them is gonna be the one that you like best. In your heart, you can like anybody you want but nobody have to know. One little girl used to come to me and say, "Who do you like better, me or my brother?" You know what I'd tell her, "Your brother." Then he used to come to me sometime and ask me who do I love better. I'd say, "Your sister." But both of them knew I was only teasing them. You don't let them know you like one better than the other one. You can't let them know.

None of my nephews and nieces know who I love best. Some I love and some I could do without but I don't let them know that. I don't hurt them. I make them think that I love all of them just about the same. But I don't.

If I had gotten to be a mother, I would have made sure my kids were loved but I would not have given them everything they asked for unless they did little chores around the house. I've known kids to get out of their beds and just go. Their parents let them. You would not leave my house if your bed was not made. Even if you were going to school, you wouldn't leave unless your bed was made. Because I'd make you get up early enough for that. You never see a bed unmade in my house. Never. I don't go nowhere with my bed unmade and my children wouldn't have done it either. It's what you teach them. And if you let them get up and walk out without the bed being made, they gonna be married and do the same thing with the others. I really would have been a good mother and my kids would have gone to school and my kids would have loved me too. Because a kid loves you even when you can't give them everything you want if they know you do the best you can. Sometimes poor kids have a better thing going for them than kids that get everything they want.

I was talking to somebody the other day and I told her to come by and have some lunch with me and just sit and watch the soap operas. But I said, "No kids. No kids." I can't sit up there and watch my soaps and be saying, "Put that down," or "You stop that," or "Come on now and sit down." I have the patience but when it's kid time, it's kid time and when it's grown-up time, they shouldn't be there. I don't like it if there's kids around when this grown-up thing is doing because you can't talk like you want to. You might want to swear every once in a while but you got to always think about the kids. And I'm not ever going to say anything bad in front of a kid. Never. Never.

WOMEN AND MEN

When I was growing up, you better not say anything about sex. You didn't ask no questions then. You didn't ask, "Momma, how do you get to be a momma?" or "Momma, where do babies come from?" You couldn't ask those kind of questions; you had to be very careful what you said. In those days, when we started getting a little sassy around the pants, they'd say, "Keep your dress down . . ." But they didn't want to tell you why we should keep our dress down. And you couldn't ask. Today, you hear what kids say on the TV talk shows and all about what thirteen-year-old kids are doing. You know you couldn't do that when I was coming up. Your mother would kill you.

Now the little girls, when they get ready to see the little boys, they're gonna get there regardless of whether the mother wants it or not. One day, a girl gets that feeling—you know what I mean—but when she comes to talk, the mother won't sit down and tell her what is what. That's why some of them girls get in trouble, because the mother won't talk to them. Some mothers don't want to talk about sex with their kids. They want to think that sex don't exist. But it exists. Don't let nobody fool you. So you got to listen to the kids, and you better talk to them. Somebody's going to talk to the kids, so if you don't talk to your kids, they gonna hear it only in the street.

One boy at school down home said to me, "You know you can say anything you want but if we go in the woods today, I know I can take some." So I said, "Okay, let's go in the woods." He had a mother and a father and he used to dress real nice. I about tore him up. I ripped all his clothes off. Boy, when that guy went home, he had something to tell his parents. He was ashamed to come back to school and tell it. I never had any more trouble with him.

In my day, the girls played all the games the boys did, like shooting marbles, batting the ball, throwing things to see who could throw the farthest, and running to see who could run the fastest. I could beat a lot of the boys. You could do all of that until you started liking boys. When you got a little older and you started liking the boys, you had to cool it and let the boys beat you at games. Even though you could do things better, you still had to let them do it better than you. I tell you I used to get so mad. I really could ride a bicycle, but once I let this boy beat me in a race because I really liked him and I didn't want to beat him. So I laid back and let him beat me. If I had beaten him, he wouldn't have wanted to bother with me. The boys just wanted to beat you on everything. If you didn't let them beat you, you weren't going to have any boyfriends. I sure hope things are different now that girls have more of a say in things.

Down home, when I was a little teen just beginning to be around little boys and feel it—you know what I mean—there was this fella who used to work downstairs in the hardware store where I worked upstairs for the family that owned the store. He was an older man. He must've been my mother's age. Sometimes they would make him come upstairs and do the heavy lifting and maybe help move something.

The man, he had a car and said he would teach me how to drive. That really made me feel good, because I took him like you would a father figure. I thought an older man would take care of me. I didn't think he would ask me anything. I had about five lessons with him and he never touched me. He got me where I could do all this steering and turning around. I learned to steer without running into anything. I could back up the car. But it was when we were learning how to park that we got off course. We were on a road someplace and he wanted to stop the car and get out and go in the bushes.

I felt like crying, but I didn't. I just said, "Take me home. I didn't think that you would do that to me. You know you're an older man. I'm a child." I said, "Why do you want me? I could be your daughter." I think a child should be ready, you know, not you just force them into it. Because everybody knows when they're ready. You don't have to be forced.

When I asked him to take me home, he said okay, and that was the end of the lessons. If he hadn't done what he did, I would probably be driving today because I was good at it. He got married right after he was teaching me to drive. He married a young girl, maybe a year older than me. I knew her at school. I met up with him years later when he moved to New York. We got to be friends again. I would speak to him when I saw him in the street.

I never told anybody about him and the bushes. Like if any one of my sisters' husbands would fumble me or something like that, if they would touch me, I would keep it to myself. I wouldn't tell my sister. (It never happened, I'm just making the point.) Because if I tell my sister, she's not going to believe me. She's going to believe her husband. If I tell, then the husband is mad at me and the sister is mad at me. So how could I go and visit them?

I'd just make sure that if he ever did it again, I'd hit him with something. And I wouldn't let her know anything about it because the woman will always believe the man. And why would I want to go to my sister's house if her husband don't like me 'cause I done told something on him. I'd rather have him like me too much like that than I'd go back and tell her that he made a pass at me. I wouldn't do that to my sister. I love her too much.

A crowd of us teenagers, boys and girls, used to go out. Once, when I must've been about sixteen, I went someplace where there was a sand hill. I don't know how the sand got there but that hill was real high and real wide. From the highway, it looked like a white mountain. The boys and girls used to go up there. This couple could be around here and that one could be around there. And they'd say to me, "Freddie, ain't you gonna get out of the car?" And I'd say, "No, not right now." Those old boys, they wanted to mess around. I was determined that I wasn't going to get no baby. At that time, they wasn't talking about no condoms or all that kind of stuff. Maybe the grown-ups talked about it but the young people didn't. And I thought of all the babies coming around and I said to myself, "No. No. No. Not as far as I'm concerned." My girlfriends would say, "You know what we did. But you never want to get out of the car. What's wrong with you?" And I'd say, "Nothing." It just wasn't my time to want to do that.

Some of my friends got pregnant. I guess them and their parents took care of the kids. But I think it's worse now than it was in my time, with little girls, fourteen, fifteen, sixteen and up to seventeen, having babies already. They're not married. Sometimes they're seventeen and they already have three babies. I want to know where's the husband. If it was me, I would just say no. Nobody had to take care of my kid, because I didn't get one. I said, "No way will I get one. There's gonna be a daddy and there's gonna be a momma." I thought, "If I'm going to do to somebody, we're going to stick." And I meant it.

I was sixteen when my mother died and I was scared to death. I was with my mother for only four years of my teenage time. I was scared that somebody was gonna get me, because I wasn't a bad-looking chick. The way I protected myself was that I fought. Since I was raised up around boys, I knew exactly how to protect myself. You know the fellas want you to cooperate and if you fight, they're not going to enjoy it. My brothers might have protected me but I didn't tell them I was fighting. I just let everything be cool.

When I started courting—that little puppy love they call it—I used to do a whole lot of fighting. But after I got grown, I stopped fighting because I wanted to be taken out: to go dancing or go to the movies and maybe neck a little. But the first place they wanted to go was to a motel. Anytime I was with a guy, like when we first started, that was what he wanted to do right away. I didn't want to go to no motel. That looked like he was just going out with me for that. I'd say, "If you go with me, there ain't gonna be no one-night stand." They'd all say, "If you like me, then why can't we . . . ?" And I said, "I'm going to have to know you awhile. If you can't wait for me, then you don't need me." I said, "If we can't go out and have a good time and instead it's gonna be bed all the time, you can forget it." I turned down a lot of dates because of men turning out to be like that.

I was a little frisky with the fellas when I was eighteen or nineteen: I was a big tease. If they start something when we are out in the car and you say no to them, they're not going to be able to get back up again. So I was safe. Sometimes I just played around. Sometimes I'd get them very frustrated, and they used to get mad. They'd cry. I was surprised that they just couldn't take it, but they couldn't because I was kind of tough. I don't know why I did that. Do you ever know why young people do things? I think I did it to get away with it. I was very, very good. They'd say, "Why you do this to me?" I'd say, "Let's go in and dance." But they weren't so particular about doing no dancing just then.

I found out that if a fella seems to like you and you say no, he gonna still keep after you. He might wait and you might wind up being his main girlfriend because you said no. I would say no for a long time and then when I would do it, the fella appreciated it. You know what I mean. Because it wasn't somebody who said yes right away.

There was one fella who waited and waited for me. He started asking me when I was about twenty-one into twenty-two. I made him wait about six months, then I decided to give up. But it wasn't like I thought it was going to be. I didn't think it would be like that unless he really didn't know what he was doing. Or I didn't know what I was doing. One of the two. I was disappointed because I thought it was going to be something different. But I waited and he treated me like a lady and that's what I want. And when I did do it, we went together for quite a spell. We didn't talk about marriage. I didn't want to. I wasn't ready.

I didn't like to have just one boyfriend. I don't mean I went to bed with a whole lot of men, but I liked to have more than one friend unless I made up my mind that I wanted to go steady. One thing about me is I like to be with people where we have fun together. Some people think you can't have no fun unless you're in bed. That's why so many marriages are not good, because the people can't have no fun together unless they are in bed. But there's more to life than that. If that was all, you can forget it because it don't last but a few minutes anyway.

You got to hold each other. You got to make fun. You make fun of each other to yourselves. All of that makes what I call love. A man and woman in the house together, that should be enough, that you want to talk and have some fun and you love each other, then you neck a little.

You should try to know each other before you get married. If you think you gonna change somebody after you get married, you can forget it. This goes for people that are white, black, blue, and green. Don't try to make nobody change, 'cause if somebody wants you bad enough, they'll change for a few minutes or for a few hours just to get what they want. And when they get what they want, they gonna be right back to where they were before. Don't try to change nobody but try to learn about them. Hang around them and see what they're like. See the person that they are.

I could've gotten married because I courted for a long time. There was one guy I met in Jersey who I really did like. He was a professional musician who played in a trio with drums and bass. He could really play the piano. He worked in the night-clubs out West and everything. Me and my girlfriends used to go out to dances and go to parties and dance a lot. But he was a musician so he didn't do any dancing. And I would go to these dances and he'd get very unhappy because I'd dance every dance from the time I walked into that place until the time came to go out. When they played that last piece to go, I'd still be dancing out the door.

He asked me to marry him but I didn't want to on account of his mother. His mother didn't like me but let's not say I didn't like her. I can get along with people because I like everybody; I don't have no picking and choosing. He was an only child and he had finished school. But his mother didn't think I was good enough for him. She told me, "You didn't finish school." I said, "What difference does it make whether I finished school or not? If I marry him, he's my husband. Let him provide for me." And I said, "I still can work because somebody will always be able to hire a cook especially when you know how to cook. And I can really cook anything I want. Anything." So she and I stopped talking for a while.

I didn't stay long with him. He said we would move out of New Jersey and we could go anyplace, but I said, "You would have to leave your mother and she would always be bothering you." If the fella's mother don't care for you, it's gonna be hard on you. Once you're going to be a mother yourself, your kids are going to be that woman's grandkids. So when he asked me to marry him, I said no, because I knew there would always be trouble.

The one I stayed with longest was James. We were together for twenty years. He was seven years older than me. When I met him, I was about twenty. James didn't live in New York; he was living in Washington. We got to be friends through his sister, who was a friend of mine. He went back to Washington after we first met, but then he came over to New York and stayed. I don't know if it was because of me. I never asked him.

James was working in Washington but I didn't know exactly what he was doing at first. I really don't think it's your business if you meet somebody to ask what they did before you met them. That's the way I feel about it. You can't say, "Oh, I'm not gonna go with him because he had a wife before he met me . . ." It's not your business what he had before he met you. And he never did say, "Well, I had a wife or I had this or the other." I didn't question him, because if he wanted to tell me he would have told me. But he never did. So I figured there was nothing to tell. 'Cause I didn't tell him what I did.

James and I were friends for twenty years. We hung out together, and oh, my God, we had a good time. Believe it when I tell you. James really was a lovable person. He was pretty handsome. He was my type, a big guy. I never did like somebody I'm looking down on. I don't like no little man. I like them bigger. I want somebody I got to look up to, somebody that can take care of me.

James could have been a boxer, and he really wanted to be one. But I talked him out of it; it really would have messed him up. I said, "Honey, somebody could knock you out and get you out of your mind and you won't know where you are coming or going." I said, "It's bad enough being a sportsman, like in basketball, football, or whatever you play. But once you get hurt, you and I couldn't be the same anymore because it would make you mean." I said, "If you my man and you got hurt, I can't just walk out on you, you know. But I can't take mean people." I talked him out of boxing. And do you know, James thanked me for that right before he died. He thanked me.

The whole while we was together, James worked as a bartender in a nice bar in Harlem. Sometimes I'd go there in the evening. I don't drink but I'd just sit in the bar and talk to him. He didn't drink much himself, not enough to get out of it. He'd take a little highball and things like that in the house but he would hardly ever drink in the bar.

We got along fine. We just went everywhere together. We went to dances, and he could dance very well. We went to Coney Island. When he wanted to go someplace, I went with him. When I wanted to go someplace, he went with me. We never had any arguments or fights; we just had fun and we never talked about no marriage. I really did care about him but not enough to say, "Let's get married." We were acting like we were but we never went to say we were gonna get married.

I liked his mother. I liked his sisters. I liked everybody in the family. Nobody said, "Get married." They wouldn't do that, not to me. Because I didn't leave an opening for them to do that. My family knew him but nobody would put pressure on me, because they know it wouldn't work. Nobody can tell me when I should get married and when I shouldn't get married.

It ended when he died. James was only in his late forties when he died, I think it was a heart attack. He had chest pains through the years but nothing too great. The doctor didn't come up with a reason why he died. Even if you die with something else, when your heart stops, if that ain't a heart attack, I don't know what is. When your heart is beating, you're still alive. When the heart stops beating, you're dead. A heart attack is what I thought when James died and left me.

I don't be living with nobody. I have never lived with anybody, including even James. I want my place to myself. I want him to go to his place and I come to mine. If I want to come and stay with somebody I wouldn't stay a period of time but only overnight. I wouldn't mind if you spend a night, but I don't want your clothes to be in the closet. You want to stay one night with me, you can, but you do not put your clothes in my house, because I will not have it.

You want to know why the fellas can't stay? Because when many ladies let men they're not married to stay, the men wind up running those ladies out of their own home. They come to stay and it winds up that she has to get out. The man harass her so much that she has to get out. It's not going to happen to me. I say the woman's home is hers. I can be alone in my house anytime I want. I pay the rent so aren't I allowed to be alone if I want to?

I said I got no reason to be married if I ain't gonna make no babies. Because that's what marriage is for. Now I done got too old that I would want to make some babies and nobody would want me now unless I get one of them million dollars from winning Lotto. Then a young fella would come and talk about how he in l-o-v-e with me. And I'd be so money-crazy, I'd fall for it. Then maybe I'd get married. But until then, no way. I don't have anything to offer, not now. Maybe if it was fifteen or twenty years ago. . . . I done give up on men now, because if you try to get somebody, it would have to be a younger man and I never did care for somebody younger than me.

One time, we had this little get-together in my house. There was three guys altogether, a younger girl, and a lady about my age. It was enough that we could be paired off if you wanted it. One of the fellas was younger and he was trying to get me. Some fellas just feel that if you're alone, you're asking for something. But I'm the type of person who doesn't want you to think that because you're a man, everybody wants you. Because everybody doesn't want you. You know where I'm coming from?

So they start drinking, and this young fella, he's getting so high. He's got this very limber hand and it just don't stop moving. It goes all over me. He's touching me and the hand falls where he want it to fall. I said to him, "No. No. No. You don't do that." He said, "Well, you're a woman." I said, "Sure, I'm a woman but I'm not your woman. I don't care if you're a man and I'm a woman. You are not my man." And I said, "I'm trying to be nice to you because you're in my home."

Well, that fella had another drink and he got so out of it. I said, "I think you had enough." He said, "What you mean I had enough? You don't tell me when I had enough." I said, "Hold on. If you want to drink some more, you gonna have to go somewhere else and get it. You gotta leave." That's one thing about me. I can put men out just as soon as I can put women out. I put him out and I never did have any more problems with that fella.

Back home nobody had a fancy wedding when they got married. When you got no money, you just got married. Sometimes you would go to the courthouse and they would take care of it. Sometimes the preacher could take care of those things but you still had to go to the courthouse and sign the book. Then you came back to the house and had some food.

And people stayed together longer then than they stay together now. Some people have big weddings now and big weddings cost good money. They spend thousands and thousands of dollars—where a gown cost two and three thousand dollars—and they stay married for only six months. They have this big wedding and six months later the man may say, "She made me mad and I just walked out." But you spent all that money for this big wedding and that don't make any sense.

You just be showing off. Showing off ain't never put no potatoes in your pot. The only way you're going to get the potatoes in the pot is to go and get them and put them in there. What they could do is just go ahead and have a little wedding. All that money they had for that wedding, I think it's better to put it in the bank. Get a little church and a little church wedding and few friends and a little eating. Take that money and go on start with a little house. And just live.

I promised that if I ever got married, it was going to be for keeps. Just like friends. I don't have a friend for just three or four years. All my friends that I have right now are people I knew before I was even a teenager. I really believe I would have made somebody a good wife. I always did say that if I had gotten married, I would be with my husband today. My first husband would be my last husband because I would have stayed with him and raised the kids if we had any. I don't have a husband but I know my man would be loved and I don't care what nobody says 'cause I'd love him. I'd really love him.

I know that marriage is a two-way street. Let's say you get married to somebody. You know if he go out and do a little something—like maybe go with another woman—I wouldn't care. I would give him another chance because it's according to what we had done through the time before that happened. Like we really loved each other. Maybe we had a couple of kids. If I would give him this chance and treat him right, me and him could talk about it and fix it together.

I wouldn't let one mistake break up what I have. I don't think he would do it again. I don't think he would make two mistakes. If you break it all up, he gonna have to take some and you gonna have to take some. But I think there's a way to keep it together, to make things last. There is a way to keep things going. You just have to try. You try to be good to each other.

When it came to me getting married, I didn't trust the men for marriage. And I just didn't love anybody enough to say I was going to make it my life. I like having fun too much to marry somebody, because he would want to stop me from my fun if I get married to him. Am I gonna get married when I can go if I want to? I'm not barricaded in no place with no guy who's gonna tell me when I can come and when I can go. And when I stay out overnight, I can stay overnight. When I want to come back, I come back. I'm not tied down to anybody. I'm free. Nobody asks, "Who were you out with?" Or "Who did you do something with?" I won't be badgered like that. What difference does it make when I walk in the door where I've been or who I was with? Don't ask me no questions. Don't ask me where I've been or who I've been with.

I think that a lot of it had to do with Pop. Your early experience injures you; some things you will not outgrow. I can't put it all on my father because I should've forgotten it, you know, but I just figure how it would be if I got married and had four or five or eight little kids and the man would walk, you know what I mean? And every time I think about it, it turns my stomach. My momma should've killed him. But she was a sweet woman. She let that bastard live. One thing you got to give her credit for was that she didn't turn us against him. She didn't say anything good about it and she didn't say anything bad about it. We were never told why he left. We had to make up in our own minds how we felt.

Some years back, Margaret and I were talking. She said, "Freddie, you know I can't understand you. You said that you really would've liked for Poppa to be around, that you missed having him. I don't understand why you feel like that." I said, "Well, I always felt like if I'd had a dad, I would have been a daddy's girl." You know how it is; there's a momma's boy and a daddy's girl. I love to get up on men. I like to sit on their laps and hug them. I didn't have that with my father and that's what I would've liked to have done: get right in his lap and hug him and look him in the eye and tell him that I love him.

But like I said, some things have to be laid aside. I'm not saying you're going to forget it. So I had to push it aside and keep on going, because if I didn't, it would've caused me to never be friends with a man, you know, much less to get married. So after I forgave my father, I got to be much more friendly with fellas than I was years back. Yes, I got to be much more friendly but I couldn't get married. I couldn't deal with it. I just couldn't. Somewhere in the way back of my mind, my father's leaving was always there. So I said, "Let me keep on playing."

If people ask, "Are you sorry that you didn't marry?" I say, "No, I'm not. Not at this age." They ask me am I sorry that I don't have kids. I say I'm not sorry that I don't have kids and I'm not sorry that I don't have a husband. I say, "Not now, because I'm so set in my old ways." But don't get me wrong. I say, "God bless the ones that marry." Don't think that I'm putting them down.

All my sisters, they got married; every last one of them. And Willie and Henry got married too. Nobody's single but Julius and me. When Julius says he'll get married when I do, I say, "Well, brother, then you're not gonna get married, because I'm not gonna get married."

How do you know what is good for you? You don't know until you try. You didn't know when you met your husband whether he was going to be good for you or not. Because the first marriage didn't work for my sister Victoria; this is her second. I went over to visit them in Philadelphia one weekend some years ago. Her husband was still working and he didn't get in until about twelvish. When he came in, I pretended to be asleep. Victoria said, "Oh, hi. Hi, baby." And they started talking. She would tell him something and he would bust out laughing. He would tell her something and she would do the same thing. And I enjoyed their conversation so much. I said to myself, "Lord, have mercy. That's the kind of man I would really like."

I know Margaret was a difficult person but that didn't

mean nothing to her husband. Maybe she wasn't difficult to him. Maybe she was sweet to him. Maybe he couldn't see how she was. Who knows? You can never tell what happens in a person's house. I don't know. I wasn't there. He was a nice guy. He let it go in one ear and come out the other. She used to tell me that he couldn't hear. I told her, "Yes, he can hear too." The same thing that happened to him happened to me. You just play deaf around Margaret, that's all. You just don't hear if you don't want to.

Margaret's husband drank a lot, maybe because she didn't want whiskey in the house. If he sneaked it in there, she'd pour it out when she'd find it. And that wasn't fair. I would've done it a bit differently. If you got a husband and he works and you know he likes a little nip, you got to have a little corner for him someplace in your house. That's what you got to do for your man, have a little corner. I don't care how small your place is, you can have some kind of little corner with some whiskey, wine, some ice, some sodas. You let that guy drink at home and enjoy himself. If he gets high and falls down, he's home. If you can't pick him up and put him in the bed, you can cover him up on the floor.

But if you tell your guy, "You ain't bringing no liquor in here and if you bring it in here, I'm going to throw it away," and then if he brings it and you pour it down the toilet and all, how do you reach the guy? When he goes out, he's gonna do just like the preacher's daughter do. The preacher won't let her go out and when she does go, she does more than the girl that was out there every night. So I think you should try to fix it for him when his dinner is almost ready and everything, that he have his little highball first. Then maybe he won't drink too much.

Sometime you make a man a drunk. If he's out there, he'll try to get it all in before he gets home because he can't bring none home. So he'll just bring what's in him. Maybe he drank a lot to make sure he had enough to come home with. If you just treat him right, I believe he can pass that by. But if you don't let him, he's gonna do till he can't do no more and then he'll come home. You know there are ways that people turn out to be drunks.

And I think that every once in a while you should let some of your husband's friends come in and you give him the house. A man just don't want to be with you all the time. He and his friends might want to play cards. They might just want to talk. I say, give him a chance to have his friends there. A man could be someplace doing something and the other men could call each other all kinds of old things and nobody would put up a fist. Then a woman would walk in there and if they call that man the same thing they did before, the men would fight.

And the wife should have a chance to have her lady friends in too. 'Cause there are things that you want to say in front of a lady that you wouldn't want to say if a man was there. You'd be too embarrassed. Everybody should have a chance to have some friends in the house to just say and do what they want to do.

You could go to a party and you could have a boyfriend or a husband there and he might start having a good time. If you say, "Oh, why doesn't he sit down?" Then everybody's gonna think the same that you're thinking. But when he's your man and when he get up there, you can say, "C'mon, baby. C'mon, do it for Momma. C'mon, get it, baby." That way everybody's going to be with that guy. Everybody. I always say, "My, my. C'mon, let's get it, Poppa," and all that kind of stuff to make him feel good. You got to make the guy feel good but if you put him down, what do you expect the others to do? If you make him feel like he's a nobody, then you're gonna embarrass him and that's when he takes off.

Embarrassment makes people do things that they shouldn't do. I will not embarrass you unless you're trying to embarrass me. Now if something happens and I come over to you, I will whisper so that only you hear. I will say quietly, "I don't like

what you did. I think you could have done it better than that."
Or, "You shouldn't have done that to me."

Some people make trouble. Sometimes when you see a man beat up on a woman, it's wrong, but it may be something she could have avoided. Let's say you are out to a party, a show, or whatever. And your husband might say, "Honey, let's go." And you are talking with some people. You start squawking, "Oh, no. Why we got to go now?" And he says, "But, honey, we got to go." And you say, "No, no. We're not going now." But all you got to do if you don't want to go then is walk him off on the side and say to him quietly, "Let's stay a little longer." Then he might say yes.

You don't shame him. You don't embarrass him. You make him feel like he is wanted. If you show him up, if you embarrass him, he might hit you. He just might. Lots of women get beat up because they shamed the man. Embarrassment brings out the worst in people. All the woman got to do is just walk the man over a little bit and say, "Let's not go yet."

If the man would try to hit me, I could stop that in the bud. If a man hits you once, it's his fault. If he hits you twice, it's a fault that is also yours. When that bastard hits you the first time and he didn't kill you, don't give him that second time. Some women are scared of men like that. They stay because they're scared to leave or because he is harassing them. He may be following them everywhere they go and everything. But I would turn the tables. I'm not gonna let him beat me. I'd just have to get it the first time. Then I would turn those tables.

You gotta make sure you make that guy think. If I wanted to still keep that man even though he hit me, I'd let him go to sleep and while he's sleeping, I would get me a baseball bat and I would belt him. I wouldn't want to hurt him too bad! I'm not a cruel person; I wouldn't hit him to blind him. I would just tie him up in a sheet and almost break his ankles. When he gets up and is ready to walk, he'll say to himself, "I know I better not bother that woman no more." You know what I mean. The first time he beats me, he'd better kill me because he'll remember me the longest day he lives every time he gets up to walk. And he'll say, "Oh, boy, that woman . . ."

You should be in a conversation with me when men start saying they think a man is smarter than a woman. They always say that a woman don't know anything. That makes me mad because it's a lie. And I can prove it.

I say that in the Bible, it was written that there was only one man, Adam. Adam stayed in the garden with a fig leaf over him. He didn't know what the hell to do with what he had. He didn't know what it was all about. But God had also wanted to make a woman, and He had already made Eve. She was the one who gave Adam the apple. But he still didn't know what to do with what he had. Eve had to tell him. All of a sudden, Adam knew everything. Then, after Eve came and told him, he said, "Oh, I know more than you." But why did he keep it there all the time and didn't do nothing with it until Eve had to come along and tell him what to do? She said to Adam, "You don't know more than me. I done told you what it was. You didn't even know. You thought it was a snake."

The best thing you can do when you sit down and talk this question out is, don't say anything about either side, man or woman. 'Cause if you put a woman down, I'll get on your case in a minute. I don't care who you are. You are not going to put a woman down in front of me. Because I know whether you white or whether you Chinese or whether you black, you got the same thing I got. You ain't going to talk bad about no woman, because I am one. If you get by putting a woman down, you're putting me down, too. And I'm not gonna let you put me down. I'll get on you like white on rice. I'm not going to let you get away with it, regardless of who you are.

Once when I was young and playing saxophone, we had a

date to play at an auditorium. Lots of church people were there; preachers and everything. The other girls in the band were eating in the auditorium kitchen. I wasn't eating so I was out there with the men. And what did they come up with but talking about women. They were saying that a man is better than a woman and all that kind of jive, that a woman is just good for staying home and making babies. I took it as long as I could take it. Then I got up there with my big mouth and told them off. And that night, I played my sax better than I ever had.

I believe you just don't down people. You don't down the man. You don't down the woman. I know a man can be a good man and he can get a lousy wife. I realize that but you just don't down each other. It's not right. I'm not going to let you say it in my company and then I won't say anything about it. They say that when you talk with men, you should go along with them, but I don't go along with them on everything. I'll put my two cents in because I have knowledge. I know right from wrong and if you're wrong, you're wrong. I don't care if you're my mother. I would tell my mother if she was right or she was wrong.

And I don't think that a woman should sit in a gentleman's company and low-rate another woman. If you low-rate me with that man, you're low-rating yourself, because you're a woman too. Why could you sit with them if they want to talk about a woman and you let them talk but you're not supposed to talk? And I've been in so many arguments about that. Someone might be saying, "That woman was no good." I would say, "What do you mean she was no good? What about the man? Why couldn't he be no good?" I say, "The woman didn't do it by herself. She had to have somebody to do it with."

I think that a woman and a man should be a man and a woman together. If there's a job a woman can do, I know she can do it, but I don't believe they should give it to her *because* she's a woman. But if she can do it, why shouldn't she get paid good money for it? That's what I'm talking about. It ain't got nothing to do with women's lib. I tell you one thing, if a woman turns out to be president of the United States, you know that war would stop. Because women ain't supposed to want to see their sons going and coming back with their heads cut off and their arms and legs cut off and all that kind of stuff.

Like I said, I think a woman is much smarter than a man.

FRIENDS

You know how there can be a gang of kids where one is more outgoing than the others? Well, that was me. When I was a little kid, I loved to hug and kiss. I was the one who grabbed my brothers and sisters. I'd just run and hug and kiss them before they had a chance to run to me. They didn't start it much; it was like they were embarrassed or ashamed. But they'd be glad when I did it. I'm just a kisser. I'm a person that's a lover. That's why when I meet my brother in the street and when I used to meet my sister, I'd kiss them, but not in the mouth. You only kiss your man in the mouth.

Some people don't know how to hug and kiss. I don't understand that. I'm crazy about people. I don't care who you are. I don't care who loves who. I don't care what the world is like. I love to love. Whether you accept it or not, that's your problem. It's not mine.

It's not what you say, it's the way you do the thing that makes people care. You might say to somebody, "I love you. I love you" and then treat them like a dog. I'd rather you don't say you love me and just treat me right. See, people don't know what love really means. Some people love cats and dogs. They just can't stand other people. They'll take a cat and a dog and just love them to death. They wouldn't give another person a beautiful smile but they will pick up a dog and hug and kiss it.

I like cats and dogs but if I had to choose between human beings and a cat and a dog, I'd take human beings. People is something that you can talk to. You can tell the dog, "Come over here" or "Get over there," and he's not going to talk back to you. I'm not saying you shouldn't love a dog, but love people too. I want to treat people in a way that they can like me. I'm gonna treat them so nice, it looks like it would kill them not to be nice back to me. I'd be so kind to them till they couldn't be mean.

When I say I like people to like me, I don't mean I'm getting under nobody's feet for them to step on me. I'm not a follower. If I have a friend and she wants to do something and I want to do something else, we have to compromise. She has to do what I want to do today and I do what she wants tomorrow. That's the way I get along with my friends. You're not going to make me do everything you want to do. I will compromise with you but when it comes around to my turn and you don't want to follow me, then I don't want no part of you.

I always got a pleasant face for people. People that don't even know me pass by and I bet they say, "God, look at that woman," and they just speak to me. I don't know what kind of a face I have, but they just speak. And I will speak to people. If I saw you in the street, I'd say, "How you doing?" I don't even have to know you, 'cause I'm gonna speak to anybody.

I don't care who you are. I'll talk with everybody: white, black, blue, or green. I will speak to you. I speak to Chinese, Puerto Ricans, Spanish. Anybody. I really don't care. We could be standing to the bus stop or something like that and I can come over and say, "Damn, it's taking this bus a long time to come." The other person might say, "Yeah, I've been here so-and-so minutes" and the next thing you know we got a conversation going. That's the way it is. People want to talk but they don't know how to start it.

The other day, I was in the subway and there was this lady

with lots of packages. She started to sit somewhere far from me, but then she looked at me and changed her mind: She came and sat down right beside me and started a conversation. I don't know anything about the lady. I never saw her before in my life. We were talking about one guy who was sitting over there. I don't know whether he was drunk or high but she said he looked like he wanted to lie down. I said, "I tell you I feel so bad for our people. We're all messed up, you know what I mean?" Then we started talking about all different things. She was going down to some street in Brooklyn. She said she liked to sit in the subway where she could be closer to the door but she sat over near me where she could hold a conversation. You know I'll never see that woman again and she'll never see me again, but for that one ride, we talked and we shared.

Another time I can get into a conversation and I wish I hadn't. Once there was a lady at a bus stop and I said, "It's taking so long for the bus and everything." She said, "Yeah, I been waiting here because I want to check on things because my landlord is gonna put me out." And she kept on about that landlord and telling me that this one did this and that one did that and the other did the other. When I tried to say something, it was like I didn't answer her right or something. She just talk, talk, talk. And when she got on the same bus that I got on, I went all the way to the back just to keep from talking anymore.

I know lots of people in my neighborhood even if it's only to say "Hi" to them. In the stores, the people always wave at me, because I'm always doing something. It's nothing that hurts you or makes you angry. I'll probably wink my eye at you or something, and then you just might wave at me.

I have people call up on the telephone and it's the wrong number. It could be a man or a woman. I say, "Hello." They say, "May I speak with So-and-so." Instead of me saying, "No, you got the wrong number" and hanging up right away, I talk sweet. I say, "Grace? Nobody in here named Grace. I'm very sorry but you have the wrong number." And they say, "Well, I sure wish it was the right number and you have a good day." And if it's New Year's or Christmas, they'll say, "You have a merry Christmas" or something like that.

Sometimes the same person that called may call right back again because they just know they got the right number. I say, "Sweetheart, you got the same person. It's a wrong number. Maybe you got a wrong digit there. Now you look up that number and see what you get, okay?" They say, "Okay. Thank you." 'Cause I have this pleasantness for people, that's what they like about it. I'm hardly ever nasty. If I get nasty, you can bet your bottom dollar that I must be sick and you better ask for help for me. Because I'm gonna try my best to be a nice old lady. That's what I really want to turn out to be.

I try to be nice to everybody. If somebody is out there begging for money and they say, "Gimme a nickel" or "Gimme a dime," some people might say to them, "Why don't you go out and get a job?" You don't have to say that if you don't want to give him anything. You could say, "I'm sorry, baby, but I don't have any money on me right now but if I had some I really would give you that nickel" or something like that.

You don't tell the guy to get a job, because maybe he wants to pick at you or say something to you because he's out for trouble anyway. So what the hell, if you're not going to give it to him, you do not have to say a thing. Or you can just say, "Baby, I'm sorry. I just don't have it today," and keep right on walking.

I like to see people laughing and enjoying themselves. I can't stand to see people tighten up. I like people happy. I love people who are friendly, having fun, not always mad all the time. You know sort of like children. Like when children watch cartoons, they are so happy.

As long as you're laughing, I'm in your party. But the minute you want to get mad, you want to curse somebody or something like that, I don't want to be in it. If we are friends, you're supposed to love me and I'm supposed to love you. You might disagree with something I say and I may disagree with something you say but there ain't gonna be any blows. Now there's some people that I'd rather not be in their company anymore, but I don't hate them; I just don't want to be with them.

When we get together, I can really bring on a party when it comes to jokes. I always go in with a bang. I can go to a party where everybody's sitting, and I walk in the door and say to myself, "Gosh, here's a dead party. Nobody is asking nobody to dance," and I say, "Why don't you put on something hot?" I go in there and shake things up and the next thing you know, everybody is dancing. They are getting down.

Then sometimes I could go to a party and everybody's having a good time but one rotten apple will come in and mess that party up. I won't let them do that.

I was at a party where a man was drinking other people's Scotch and he had brought a bottle of gin. I went over to him very kindly—and not letting everybody else hear—I said, "You know you brought gin." He said, "Yeah." I said, "Well, you shouldn't drink too much of the other people's drink." I said, "You're not drinking anything but Scotch and you brought gin. Now if you had've wanted Scotch, you should've brought Scotch but you brought gin." And I said, "You stick to your gin from now on." He didn't get rude or anything and start talking loud. The Scotch wasn't important to me but I wanted to make sure he didn't drink them other people's drink.

I will take people like that over and try to cool them down. You know before that party's over, I'll have that person right in with everybody else. I would go over to her or him and act like he's the greatest or she's the greatest. And everybody wants to be great, you know. I will tell her, "You are something else, girl. Let's go over and have a drink." I don't drink myself but

I'll probably have a soda or something like that and let them have a drink.

And if it's a man and a nice dance piece comes on—either fast or slow—I'll say to him, "Come on. Let's get some of that." And I'm gonna show off my dancing to make him feel like he's the life of the party. And before this thing is over, everybody wants to dance with him. There is no upset.

Sometimes when somebody wants to upset a party, when he gets ready to throw something, I will put up my hand and say, "You don't want to do that. That's not nice. You're not in your own home." They don't say, "Man, I sure hope she don't ever come back here again" like they do if you did something wrong. Any place I go, they walk me back home.

If I go to a place and everybody wants to say something to make somebody feel bad, I will leave. I can't get you jumping if everybody is mad at everybody. I have been places like that where everybody just don't get along.

When you want to get in a place and have a good time— even if you have a small apartment—don't worry, you'll get in there. If you want to get in and have a nice time, you'll find the space even if you have to sit on the floor. When people are laughing and talking, we have such a good time.

I don't like arguing. I have walked in places where people were discussing something. It could be the news, God, or whatever. The people might ask me, "Do you think I'm telling the truth?" I don't want you to ask me questions like that, because I don't want to be in it, whatever you're talking about. You were probably talking about it when I got there. When they say, "Don't you think I'm right?" I just tell them I don't want to be in it. 'Cause if you want to fuss, there are three things that will cause you to get in an argument: the Bible, God, and the world.

But I will get in arguments with my friends about things that happen, about what we read in the newspapers and other things. Everybody has an opinion about what they think is right. That's where the conversations come in. I'll argue about church. I'll argue about God. I'll argue about something like O. J. Simpson. My opinion is my opinion and yours is yours. You give me yours and I give you mine. Now I don't look for you to say that I'm right but don't say that I'm wrong. You can think any kind of way you want but your view is going to be yours. I'm not going to argue with you about it or anything like that. But you ain't going to make me turn over to your side. I'm not going from my figuring to yours. And I've been like that all through my life.

I keep my friends 'cause I don't fuss and argue that we got to curse each other out. If I had to curse you out, I don't want you to be my friend 'cause I love my friends too much and I can't stand all this bickering. Let's say you say something to me and I got to hit back at you. Or I say something to you and you jump right back at me. And the next time we're arguing and fussing about something. That's the way you lose friends.

Grown-ups are not supposed to fight. They're supposed to teach the kids. I'm not talking about fighting with words. You know you can hurt each other with words, but I'm not talking about that. That's mental. When I say fight, I mean probably scratching up your face. I'm talking about actually hurting each other. I don't do any of that kind of fighting anymore. I try to make peace all the time.

Nobody's gonna think like you think. If you think one way, somebody else gonna think another way and that's where the bickering gets in. I might say, "I don't believe he did that" or "I think he did do it." I can look at a person's face and see that he's really getting angry. If you know how to read a person, you can almost tell when you've irritated him. Then I say, "Maybe he did that. Maybe he did do it." So that satisfies them and you can see that expression moving off their face. I don't have to argue with them about it. I said what I think it is. If I say, "I think he did it" and you say, "I don't think he did it," then it's up to you to keep the argument going because I'm finished with it. So if you want to keep arguing, that's your problem not mine.

I'm in the street and I meet somebody—a friend now, not just anybody. It could be a him or a her and we're talking. And something might kind of strike a nerve, like you could be talking and say something that they may not be too pleased with, that's getting on their nerves, and they start talking loud. I don't like a scene like that. Whatever I say to them or they say to me, nobody else should know about it. If something goes wrong that they don't like, we should talk about it right there and don't let nobody else know.

I wish people could always be sweet and kind. But people will just say and do anything. They will get insulting. They will hurt your feelings. Let's say at this particular time, I don't want to go to a movie. Maybe you will say, "Oh, you don't want to go with me because you think I'm not good enough for you." I don't get mad, I explain myself gently. I don't fight with my friends. If I'm gonna get mad at you for everything you say, there's never gonna be any friendship.

And God knows I treat people so nice. If I could buy love and sell it, I could make a fortune with my love. Some people might say I'm a pushover, but I'm not. I might do things that people want me to do. But when somebody crosses me, I'm just like a black snake. I scratch. That's why I try my best to keep from letting you see that bad side of me. I can be nice but you better don't cross me. If you really push me, I could get awful mean.

I give people enough rope to hang themselves. Suppose somebody says something that I dislike. I won't just come out and say, "Oh, I don't think you should have said that to me." I won't say anything about it. But the next time we meet each other, I'm not as friendly as I was the time when you said that to me. I'm still kind to you but it's not the same kindness like it was before. It doesn't have to be cold outside but you can still freeze somebody out. Now this is the rope I'm talking about: When they get home, they will start thinking to themselves, "You know, Freddie wasn't quite as friendly today." And they say to themselves, "Ohhh, I bet she didn't like what I said." And do you know that person will never say that again. You don't have to hang them. You give them enough rope, they will hang themselves. They just know to don't say the same thing they said the time before. They will make it up in their mind that they never will say that again. If you had've stopped them or said something to them or made them feel bad like they done hurt you, that can build a fire.

One time a lady told me to kiss her ass. I brushed it off. I figured if I followed it up we would fight and it would cause a lot of confusion. I don't want it to be like that. So I wait. I think that if she happens to say it again, I'm gonna kiss her. Then she would know not to do it to anybody else.

Some people let every little thing get in the way of a relationship. I talk on the telephone with somebody and I say, "What have you heard from So-and-so-and-so?" They say, "The last time we talked, I was the one who called. And I'm not going to call again. I ain't gonna stoop that low." And I tell them, "What difference does it make who called last? Maybe she ain't thinking about you when you're thinking about her." I say, "That's your family or that's your friend." I got people calling each other that never would have called before. Sometimes I call people three times before I get a call back. I'm thinking about them. They might not be thinking about me. So my call makes them say to themselves, "Hmmm. She's thinking about me." So one day they gonna get on that telephone and say, "I bet you can't guess who this is." And it's gonna be the one that I done called three times before.

I like to stay in touch with people. We don't have to see each other. We don't have to visit each other. All we got to do is talk on the phone. Just let's find out how we're doing. You call people when you're thinking about them 'cause if you don't call, you can forget all about it. My friends know me very well. They know how I operate. They understand that I'm not going to see people all the time but that I want to know how they're doing.

I got a few friends who call pretty often; I got others who don't. But I will call you regardless. The only way I won't call you is if you tell me, "Don't call me anymore." If you tell me that, then you ain't got no more problem with me.

People will tell me, "Oh, I saw So-and-so-and-so in the street but I didn't say anything to her." I say, "Why? That's your homey! You saw her but maybe she didn't see you. You go up and let her know you see her." I say, "You dumber than she is."

When people go down South, somebody'll see them but won't say anything to them. And when you talk to that person, they'll say, "Oh, yeah. I saw him but I didn't say anything to him." Then I'll jump all over them. I say, "If you see me and I don't see you, you're supposed to hail me." But see, when you don't love or when you got that old ignorance in your head, you don't think about that. All you're thinking about is you want to be mean. But me, if I see you in the street, I'll stop you in a minute and say, "Hey, man." And they'll say, "Ohhh, Freddie Mae Baxter." That makes me feel good and you don't have to pay for that.

Some people can get along fine and then all of a sudden one little thing happens. Someone makes a mistake. They do one thing wrong and that just kills everything. That is not the way to live. People can make mistakes. And once a mistake is made, it's almost like a glass of milk that you did something with in the kitchen and it spilled on the floor. You never get that glass of milk anymore. But you got to think about the good things they've done for you. You always been such good friends through the years and now are you gonna let one little glass of milk take away all them beautiful years?

. . .

You got to give people another chance. There was one girl who did something to me. The mistake she made was real personal, so I prefer not to say what it was. She made a mistake, that's all. She can't take that back. It's made already. I was so angry when I got home. But I didn't hate her for it. I gave her another chance. She was one of my best buddies. We did everything together. I said to myself, "I'm gonna sleep on it." But I didn't even need to sleep on it; I just gave her another chance.

I may even give a person three chances but I'm not gonna give them more than that, 'cause even in a ballgame, three strikes and you're out.

Everybody's allowed to make a mistake. That's why they have pencils with erasers. Why do they put the erasers there if they don't think you'll make a mistake? They would just have the pencil. But some people don't want to forgive. They're so hurt that they just don't want to forgive. But they're breaking up a beautiful relationship.

Some people will never apologize. They'll say, "Just let them suffer." They'll tell you in a minute, "I don't care." I'm never too stout to apologize if I did something wrong. If you accept my apology, that's good. But there's some people that won't accept it. If you don't accept it, there's nothing I can do.

You get mad with somebody and that's the end of a twenty-year or a thirty-year relationship. And I don't think it's fair. Let's say you're not speaking to me. You haven't spoken to me in two weeks. You're over there and I'm over here. If I don't say to you, "What's wrong? What is it that you're so angry about?" then we ain't never gonna speak. Maybe you're too mad to come and say, "Freddie, you said this," or "Freddie, you did that." Somebody's got to give. Somebody's got to cross the line. If nobody crosses the line, then you never gonna get where you're going.

I know people on the plantations down South that stayed

mad for forty and fifty years. Like in this family and that family, nobody spoke to nobody. They stopped speaking way back there because a little incident probably happened. If you're not speaking to somebody about something, you're not going to be able to forget what they said. You can get old and gray and everything but you're still gonna remember how that one did that to you forty years ago. You ain't never gonna accept that. But the good stuff you forget. You can do something really good for a person and they just pass over it. You turn around and do something bad to him and he gonna concentrate on the bad. He's gonna forget all about that good stuff you did. That's why people don't get along today.

I was working for a family one time and there was this little boy I was taking care of. I had a friend who was working for another family and they had a little girl. I would try to let the little girl come to the house to play with my little boy. When she came, I would watch both kids and my friend was free to go and probably do whatever she want. Then when the time came to pick up the little girl, I would call her and say, "When you coming over to pick her up?"

This particular night, I called my friend and she said, "I'm not coming. I'm cooking. I got a pot on the stove. You got to bring her here." I guess my friend figured that if she didn't go, I'd bring the little girl. I call that taking advantage. I told my friend that I was cooking too, and that I had a pot on the stove. I could've said, "No, I'm not going to come." And she would've had to come and get the kid. But I went and took the little girl home. It wasn't too far, just a few blocks. And I had to take the little boy with me. I had to turn my stove off and run them couple of blocks and take that kid to keep my friend from being in trouble. I just wasn't gonna let that child be here when she was supposed to be there. I stopped what I was doing and went and took that little girl home to save my friend's job.

I said, "I could've said no and got you in lots of trouble

because them people would have wanted to know where their child was when they got home. Why would you do me like that?"

But I'm not going to let that whole thing break up a friendship. She would have to do more than that. But I told her, "I'm not going to give you no more breaks." And I didn't. You know I let the little girl play with the little boy but I made sure they played in the park.

People will fail you when they know that you never say no. I swear sometimes that you got to say no but it looks to me like I'm always saying yes. If you're a yes person, you get more to do.

I'm straight with people and I like for them to be straight with me. If I ask you, "Would you like to go to a movie?" Don't come and tell me okay, then you stand up in the line to get your ticket and look for me to pay. I'm not gonna pay for you and I'll let you know that. But if you tell me, "I don't think I can make it because I don't have any money," then I may tell you, "Oh, that's all right. I'll pay your way." And if I can't afford it when they ask me to go, I'm gonna say so. But if they say they'll pay my way, then I'll go but I won't be looking for them to pay my way.

I try to keep things on the level but I'm my own person. Let's say I'm out with my friends and everybody wants to go someplace. If I want to go, I go. If I might not want to go, I say no. Let's say it's a bar. Well, I don't drink so why should I go in there if I don't want to go in there? So I go and I do something else. I don't go away mad. And they're not going to get mad, because if Freddie says she's not going to do something, you can bet she's not going to do it. And they leave me alone. It's the same thing with the family. If they ask me something, I'm very free to go and help but if it's something I don't want to do, I say, "No, I'm not gonna do it." Sometimes I go along but it's gotta be something that appeals to me. After all, I got a life too.

I talk my tail off because people are uptight all the time. And I'm not going to hide anything from people; I'm not gonna tell you something and then tell you not to tell anybody. If I want to tell it to them, I tell it to them myself. I'm very outspoken to people and they know that.

I don't ever tell nobody, "Now don't you tell that." If you say that, you must want other people to know because every time you tell somebody to don't tell something, they gonna go ahead and tell it anyway. That gives them something to gossip about. I have close friends and I can say almost anything to them and I don't have to tell them not to tell it. I don't believe they would. I don't like that talking behind when somebody comes in and everybody shuts up. You know they gotta be talking about you or talking about something they don't want you to hear. Sometimes it will happen, 'cause why would they shut up when I walk in the door?

People can tell me anything they want and I forget about it. Then when it comes up, when somebody says, "You didn't know about So-and-so-and-so?" I say, "Are you kidding?" (Of course, I knew about it all the time but I act like I'm just finding it out.)

But I don't like to gossip. Because if I gossip with you about Miss Susan, I'll get with Miss Susan and then gossip about you. I don't like it like that. Whatever we talk about, I don't want it to hurt the next party in case somebody starts talking about it.

One of my best friends went to Florida. She's from Florida but I met her in New York. Her name is Bernice. She and I were buddies for over forty years. She was doing the same work as me and she was working near me.

Bernice is a little woman, five foot three. She was much shorter and much quieter than me. She was nice, somebody to talk to, somebody that didn't break in on you when you had something to say.

I met her when I was playing in her father's band. Bernice didn't play music at all. She came to one of the sessions that we had and I met her and we got to be friends. We did a lot of things together. We went to the movies. We went to the beach. We took bus trips together. Everywhere there was to go, we went. We used to hang out and double-date. Now this wasn't her husband that we were hanging out with. Bernice had been separated a long time ago. They never did get a divorce. Her husband was still in the South. She'd see him down there but they would just have a "hello" thing.

She's got a couple of sisters and cousins up this way but she said that when she retired, she was gonna go back to Florida. She got herself a little home down there about four years ago and she's doing all right. We keep in touch by phone and we write. She says she wished she had stayed in New York a little while longer. She misses the things that we did.

Bernice knows that I'm not going down there to visit her. We were close friends and buddies but we made a pact that if she died before me, I'm not going down there for the funeral and if I died before her, she's not coming up here. She doesn't want to see me dead. And I don't want to see her dead. We're not gonna pick up and come 'cause she done got old and I done got old. We gonna keep in touch until one of us passes and whichever one it is, the other is gonna get a nice card and send it to the family and that's all she's gonna do. We know the family will always say, "Oh, it be a shame that she didn't come to the funeral when her best friend died." But we made a pact. Ain't nobody gonna be in that pact but she and I.

Bernice had one son. His name is Richard. I knew him when he was a little boy. He was raised by a one-parent family but he would sometimes stay with his father and then come back and stay in New York. He was up here with his mother until he got grown and finished school. Then he moved out West. I know her son didn't finish college but he's doing all right for himself 'cause he's working. When you're working, you're doing all right for yourself. Some people that finished college, they ain't doing nothing. I think he's a social worker who helps little kids.

If you're my friend and you've got children, I'm gonna like your children too. Bernice's son can really charm. He always was so mannerly and he was always nice and good to his mother. He would always take her places. I would have loved to have a son like that. Every once in a while, he will write me a letter.

I believe he's the only young man I been knowing since he's a kid that I would let come into my house and I wouldn't be afraid. You know how kids grow up and they're not kids anymore. They're men and you are skeptical to have them around when you're alone 'cause you don't know what's on their mind. But Richard always loved me and I don't believe that he would say or do anything to his Freddie Mae. And any way I can help him, I'd open my home to him. Even if he wanted to sleep here, he could sleep. I would take him as if he was family. I call him a nice young man but he ain't a young man no more now. I think he's in his fifties.

Ida Mae is another friend. She's a little bit younger than me. We grew up together and went to school together. We played together and did a whole lot of things together. She's married. She got a fine-looking husband. She had eleven kids. All of them are alive. One of them had an automobile accident. She was in a wreck and hurt herself where she couldn't walk right. Outside of that, everybody is all right. Ida Mae's kids got grown. They all of them got out and married and got their own kids.

Ida Mae took care of foster kids for years. That's the way she got quite a bit of her money. In later years she adopted one of them. She lives out on Long Island. When people move out of Harlem and move to Long Island, they stay there. They try to find other friends out there.

Another friend of mine is Evelyn. She's one of my homeys from way back when we were really little. She lives in Brooklyn now. She had three boys and a girl. I speak with her two or three times a year now. She used to give a picnic every year, a big party on Labor Day in a little park near her house. She'd cook everything in the house, bring it out, and all the homeys would come to the picnic, all the men and women from our hometown. You'd get a chance to see people from home.

At the picnic, they would have radios playing different music and all of us were dancing around if we felt like it. But mostly I liked to talk and to look at them people's faces that I've been knowing all my life.

We used to have a dance every year, up here in New York, to raise money for a school down South. When I left from down there it was only a two-year college but we raised it up to four years. They had classes for everything, just like any college. And they built a trade school there. The children got where they could build furniture for their parents. One guy built his mother one of those things that you put the plates and the glasses and things in there; something like you buy with the dinette table. It had glass doors. If that school had been there when I was coming up . . . oh, boy!

Those dances for the school were really something. Sometimes you would see people that you hadn't seen since the first and second grade. One guy used to go back home two and three times a year because his mother was there. He'd go home to see his mother and when he went home, he could find out where people were at up here in New York. Once you get to know where they're at, you know how to get in touch with them and tell them to come down and be at this dance. And each one would tell the other until the whole place was packed.

And sometimes you didn't even want to dance. All you wanted to do was to hug and kiss.

The school is still running but nobody is raising money for it now. We thought maybe the younger people would keep up the dances but they didn't do it.

When I was younger, I studied people. I would watch things and see how they worked out. You could be talking and I'd just be sitting. Maybe at the end of the conversation, I would give you my view of whatever it was we were talking about. Sometimes what I had to say meant as much as the whole conversation.

But don't get me wrong, I will listen.

I was telling my niece, "You know I really believe that people bother me a lot because I listen." People can be down, down, down in the dumps, you know—like it's something they want to yell about—and they'll call me and I'll start listening to them and letting them get it out of their system. When they call and want to talk, I listen to them. Then in-between there, I might ask them a question and see what they got to say. And they'll talk and talk and talk and when they get all that off their minds, they're back to themselves again.

When people are sorry for themselves, it hurts their insides. Black people and white people too—if they feel sorry for themselves—they've got to get it off their chests. If not, you gonna have heart attacks, you gonna have strokes. Let's say you're worried about something. Long as it's kept in your mind, you feel bad. You can't sleep. And when you get it off your mind, when you say what's bothering you, you get it off. Anybody can get depressed. I didn't go to school for this, but I know I could still help somebody not go and jump off the roof, or maybe not kill themselves some other way. Because I have done it.

·   ·   ·

People call on the telephone for advice and I try to give them the best answer I can. Sometimes it might make them feel good. Sometimes it might make them feel bad.

When I give advice, I don't want them to think that I'm gonna think like them. Because two people are not gonna think alike. I might go along with what you say sometime and you might go along with what I say sometime, but if you're looking for me to tell you what you want to hear, I can't do that. I have to tell you what I think. Sometimes if you don't give people what they would like to hear, they say they don't want to talk about it.

Some people ask you something about their kids, and you try to give them your opinion. They say, "Ah, no. No. We be talking about something else." I say, "No, we gonna stay right on that subject. You asked me. If you didn't want to stay on that subject, you shouldn't have asked. And I'm gonna tell you just what I think of it."

I won't ever tell a person to leave anybody. And I don't ever say, "Why don't you beat him or her up?" I don't do that.

You can't make people do some things unless they decide they want to do it themselves. They got to make it up in their own minds, because nobody could make them do it. That's almost like a person that used drugs. You might want to send them someplace to straighten them out, but you can talk until your hair is white if they don't make it up in their own mind to go.

I always tell my friends, "Try if you can. If you don't have this or don't have the other, just leave it go. You really can do without it. You don't need to have that." Let's say Christmas is coming and you might not have enough money to buy the kids exactly what they ask for. I say, "Don't be disappointed. Get them kids what you can afford and if they don't like it, too bad." You can't get $150 sneakers for a ten-year-old boy. I say, "You know, if you can't afford them, don't get them. He will survive. His feet not gonna break off 'cause you didn't have those sneakers for him."

The hardest question I was asked was, "Should I divorce my husband?" I can't answer that one unless I know what's going on. I might like both of them and if I tell one something about that, they'll say, "Freddie said I should do so-and-so-and-so." That makes it sheer hell for the other one. Then if they get back together, I lost two friends. So I just say, "Why don't you wait and see what happens? Give him another chance and then if he did whatever he did again or something, maybe it's because things are tough out there." I say, "It's not easy to find a good man. At least he's a provider and he's probably good to the kids. After a while, the kids will be grown and going away and it'll be good for you and him. Then maybe you can make it." And sometimes they'll come back and tell me that I said the right thing.

I knew a girl that was really getting ready to leave her husband. She came to me and my girlfriend and we told her that they should stay together and we told her why. She went back and they had two kids after that. When she came to talk, they had two boys. Then they had another boy and a girl so they had three boys and one girl. Them people are right together now.

When my nephew Bubba took sick, he talked to me like he wouldn't talk to his own mother. I just knew everything about it because he knew I could hold a secret. He told me the condition he was in. He told me that the doctor told him he had to have a colostomy. That put me in a bind because I couldn't tell his mother. If I had told her, she would be screaming and hollering and carrying on, and she'd probably fall out with a heart attack. So I never told her. After Bubba was gone, his mother knew because it was on the death certificate that he had cancer.

I get down myself sometimes but my friends think that I'm never in trouble. They just think that I'm always happy-go-lucky. Most of the time, I feel fine. And when I'm happy,

I'm very happy. But sometimes I feel bad like everybody else. I know that when people call me and I say I don't feel well, they feel bad but they'd rather not talk to me. So I'm always saying, "Oh, I feel fine." And maybe I don't. I say that so they can keep their balance.

But you know, I want to talk sometimes. It's very hard to find somebody that will listen to you. People are not so particular about hearing what I've got to say. They'll listen if you get mad at them or something and you want to bitch them out. They'll listen to that more than when I'm trying to be nice and I want to talk. But so many times, they just don't want to hear what I got to talk about. They want me to hear what they have to say.

People have called me and talked; talked sometimes for an hour and a half. That takes up my time but I listen to them. I don't say, "Well, I got to go." But when I call them and we talk a little bit, they say, "Well, Freddie, it was nice talking to you." That means they are ready to get off the phone. They're turning me off after they talked to me for an hour and a half. It's almost like they done cut my throat. I get so pissed off. I done told a few people about this. I say, "If I call you and you don't have time to talk, then tell me that you'll get back to me. Don't talk a little bit, then say to me, 'Well, it was nice talking to you.'" What they should tell me is that something came up or they were cooking and they will get back to me. That would make me feel much better.

I sometimes get depressed, too, but nobody wants to hear what I got to say. When I get depressed, I call somebody and start talking and they say that that's the same thing that happened to them. They'll say, "Yeah, this morning I woke up and I had this pain all up and down my leg and my neck and my so-and-so." Or when somebody is calling me back, they done forgot that I felt bad.

Sometimes my family gets me angry. Not that I'm all that

mad, because you know we can't divorce the family. All your family ain't gonna be a good listener. But when you have a friend or a close member of a family, then you don't mind talking to them about whatever it is. If something is bothering you, you can find somebody that you can talk to, that you trust. I can't understand how some people have to go to psychiatrists. What are you going for? Why do you have to pay for it? I don't see how in the world somebody gonna pay money to go sit up and somebody let you do all the talking. The psychiatrist ain't doing any talking. You're doing all the talking. I could sit up in my house and talk to myself. You know where I'm coming from. And the kind of money that they have to pay! They pay big bucks for that thing, you know.

I don't think I'll ever need a psychiatrist. How he gonna tell me something? I know more about me than anybody knows about me. If I would go to them, they'd probably tell me to get on the couch and they gonna talk to me. If I went, I would turn this thing around. I'd tell him or her to get up there on the couch and tell me something about themselves. I'd say, "You ain't gonna know nothing about me if you ain't gonna tell me nothing about you."

I have worked with kids who had to go to psychiatrists and I said to myself, "All the mother has to do is give me that money and I'll straighten the kids out. All the kids have to do is talk to me." I really would have been good. I know I can make people feel good about themselves. I do that a lot on the phone and sometimes in person too. I say to them, "You know, I should charge y'all." If I had finished school and gone to college, I could have been a psychiatrist. If I ever had the chance to study, that would have been my trade. If somebody's in trouble or something like that and they feel like they need somebody to talk to, I could sit and listen to them and give them advice.

.   .   .

In my building, there are some old people who wake up in the morning and there's nobody to say, "Good morning. How you feel this morning?" Some people don't ever get a hug and a kiss. When I see them, I say "Hello, young lady!"

When I come out of my house, some mornings there will be old ladies sitting around there. Sometimes they wait for the mailman; sometimes they just be sitting. Well, I come out and go all the way down the line. I give each one a kiss. And you can see their faces light up like a Christmas tree. Them old ladies are sitting there and when they see me, maybe they think, "Somebody loves me." When their faces light up, my heart lights up like a Christmas tree too.

I saw an old lady from the first floor in the hallway the other day and I said, "Hi, gorgeous." She looked so surprised. We just embraced each other and everything. She said to me, "You are so pretty." I said, "Go on, girl. You sure told the truth." I saw an old lady I know coming across the street with a girl that comes to work for her. So I came around to where I could get in front of her before she crossed the street. I said, "Hi there, young lady. Where you going?" The lady was so pleased. I might be doing it for them but how they react from me doing it makes me feel good too. It's kind of like therapy for me.

Sometimes I tease them to give them a little bit of upbeat. Some of them be in their eighties or nineties now. Sometimes they be peeking under the trees waiting for the ambulette to take them to the hospital. I see them with a walking stick, and I act like I'm going to kick that stick out from under them. I tease all of them; not to say I like this one better or that one better. I pick at them and they just start laughing. That's 'cause somebody's saying something to them, you know what I mean?

One time it was all senior citizens on my floor. We were just like a family. Anything happen, everybody looks out for everybody. I am the nosy one there. I have found people's keys in their door. One time, I smelled gas. I went to everybody's door and smelled every one. When I got to one door, I start hollering, "I smell gas. I smell gas. Come on. Open your door. Everybody get out of here." One of the ladies on the floor had a key to that apartment. The lady in there had turned on all the jets on her stove. And the windows were closed and everything.

The lady had been getting kind of sick and going out of it. When you get out of it, you don't know what you doing. You don't know whether you turned the gas on or not. You could think you turned it on and then turned it off. You just don't know. The lady with the key went in and she opened all the windows. The doorman came up and checked it out. That woman finally had to go 'cause she had nobody to take care of her. She's in a nursing home now.

After working with my children, I left when they done gone to college and everything. Then I started working with older people. I can be gentle with old people. Sometimes words will come out of their mouths that shouldn't come out. They will say things because they really don't know mostly what they talking about. Some girls will not take it; they figure that old people shouldn't say that, that everything should be right on the money. Well, I have worked for people, mean old people, that other people couldn't work for. But you got to read between the lines.

Some people will take it to heart. I won't. I will walk out of the room. After I walk out—and I don't care how old they are—they gonna think about what they said. If I had turned around and said, "You got no business saying that to me. Don't you dare say that to me again!" they'd think, "I can make her mad. I'm still alive." So I always treat them in a way that they have to know that they did something wrong. I don't fuss with them. I don't curse them. I wouldn't hit them for anything in the world. Some people do; they think if the old people are mean, then you gotta be mean. I would never hit one the longest day I live. If you're mean, you're not helping them and you're not helping yourself. Even sometimes when they might want to hit you or something like that, what I do is take their hand and I rub it. I say, "Does your hand hurt, baby?"

Old people know when you're being nice to them and not being nice to them even if they're half crazy; even if they get Alzheimer's or whatever you call it. I've had doctors call me and ask me was I working with one of their patients that day because that patient was calm and friendlier than before. I don't give any needles. But the doctors liked the way I had with the old people.

If you treat them right, you can make old people do things for you without having to scold them, hit them, or whatever. It's the way you carry yourself. You can't just say, "Come on, we got to go. Let's go." You don't do them like that. You give them a chance. If they see you being so kind to them, you look in their face and you see a different expression there. Then they will do most anything you want them to do.

You're their caretaker but when you walk in, they say that you're their sister. Well, their mind is all screwed up. You don't pretend to be their sister. You leave it alone 'cause they gonna get back to themselves. But if you bug them with it, if you say, "No, no, I'm not your sister," you get them further off from what they're thinking about. If you bother them, you gonna confuse their mind. You're not supposed to upset them old people, because they don't know what they're talking about. So you walk out that room, and later on you walk back in there and you might say, "Good morning." And they say, "Oh, Freddie Mae." Their mind done come back.

You disturb people if they're trying to talk to you and you cut in instead of listening to them. Sometimes they say something and you interrupt them. You talk while they're talking.

You make them forget what they were ready to tell you. Let them finish the whole sentence; you don't know what they gonna say. Even a child might have wanted to say, "Momma, I love you."

And old people done got back to being like a child, so you got to listen and see what they're talking about. Leave them alone and let them say what they were saying. Then when they finish, you take their hand and you say, "So-and-so-and-so, I love you." Then they say, "I love you too."

My sister Margaret is in a nursing home now. At one time, she wasn't saying anything. I believe she was angry. You know, sometimes they get angry that you had to put them in a nursing home. And if they get that anger in there, you have to leave them alone for a long time until it be fished out of them. You know when you get sick, you get angry. You could talk but you just won't talk.

Not only Margaret but anybody that you have to put in a nursing home, they think they shouldn't have been put there and they'll get that in their mind and they stay mad for a while. I know that people can put you in a nursing home and don't come back no more. That's what makes people go out of it and die. Maybe they worked all their life and probably left some kids or grandkids back there. Then they go in a nursing home and nobody comes to see them. You can go crazy like that. Now you thinking, "I worked all my life. My money is out there and they gonna be using my money. But I'm sitting up in here. They could come and sit and talk with me. Let me look at them at least."

And Margaret would sit up there and not be talking. That bothered me. I said, "Sis, why won't you talk to me?" And she said, very quiet, "I got nothing to talk about." She wasn't saying anything, just sitting up there like a statue. She didn't seem to care. She wasn't saying a word. I'd say, "Maggie." She'd say, "Hmmm." I'd say, "Why don't you talk to me?" She'd answer, "I ain't got nothing to say." And that's all she would say the whole time I was visiting her. When I went to see her, I would lay back in my chair and think about it for a little while. I could see that her tongue was beginning to get heavy. (If you stop talking, you're not going to be able to again because your tongue gets heavy.) I said to myself, "I see what's going on. I'm going to have to change some things around here and do some more talking." So I just sit there and talk to myself.

The way I talk, I think I can talk a dead man alive. I just talk, talk, talk. Most of the time the way I got started is to say, "You know I'm trying to think of that guy's name." I think his name was Johnny but I can't think of his last name. And Margaret says, "I know what the last name is. I know. Do you mean Johnny Attbury?" You know I'll bring up them kind of things and I'll act like I don't know anything about it.

Every time I would go, I would always bring up something from way back then. And she'd say, "Oh, yeah." She can't think of things that happen a year ago or six months ago, but she can tell me some things from way back there that I think I've forgotten about. And I try to make her tell me what this was all about. Margaret talks about different people from way back when. And I know she's telling the truth because I know the people and I know they did whatever she says they did. And you can see she's way back there, coming this way. She's coming back.

You know Margaret's doing pretty good now. At least she's talking again. She holds a conversation with me. We're talking heavier and heavier. She's just like a talking machine now. Me and my sister be there laughing. She'll laugh and talk and tell me about things I done forgot about. She'll say, "Do you remember So-and-so-and-so? Do you reckon she's still alive?" And if they're not alive, I tell her. I don't say, "Oh, leave it alone," 'cause she's doing good enough for you to tell her that they're not alive now.

One day I went there and she said she didn't want the

nurses to do anything for her. She told me that her daughter brought her some sweet potatoes and she wouldn't let none of the nurses take them, so they stole her sweet potatoes. I knew it didn't happen—her daughter never comes—and that Margaret probably had a dream. So I had to get her calmed down. And I did. We started talking about things that I had almost forgotten about, things that went way back. She was all right when I left.

Thank the good Lord, Margaret is doing better now; she's coming back. She still can't get out of bed on her own but she will let them sit her up, let them move her on the side of the bed for them to help her. She'll stand up so they can get clothes on her. Recently she was telling the nurses that she didn't like that dress and would like to put on another one. Before it was whatever they put on her, she didn't care.

She's watching the TV now, where she wasn't watching no TV before. When I'm up there, I usually try to turn on "Soul Train" for her; that's where those kids are dancing. I think mostly she likes the cartoons. When I get ready to leave these days, she'll look at me and say, "Oh, I sure wish you didn't have to go." That makes me feel so good, like it's an uplift for me. When I walk in now, she grabs me and wants to hug and kiss me. Before, she would just be sitting there.

Margaret can't ask questions about the present. She hasn't talked about her apartment or her clothes or anything like that but she talks about little things that let me see she's coming back. One day she said, "I sure would like to go home with you." She didn't say to her home, although she don't know that she don't have a home now. (We had to give up her apartment.) I swear to God, I don't know what the hell I'm going to say if she asks about going to her apartment, because she wouldn't have been able to take care of herself properly there. She would have to have somebody around the clock and we can't afford that.

HARLEM

I have never lived anyplace in New York but Harlem. The first building I lived in was on 120th Street.

I had my own place but I had roommates. I had one roommate who stayed with me a long time. She did the same kind of work I did but mostly she worked with old people. We didn't mix our things together. She had what she did and I had what I did. If her boyfriend came, I'd go. If mine came, she would go. We didn't have no problems.

I liked the way we handled ourselves. We didn't fight. We didn't fuss. We had no problems when it came to paying the rent. She was really good about that. With some people, when time comes to pay the money, they have a little spat. They say, "I was mad at her so I didn't give her any money." But that's not the point. You can't say that if you're mad at me, you ain't gonna give me the money. Whether you're mad at somebody or not, you put that money on the table in an envelope that says "Rent" on it.

After living in rooms for a while, I got a place of my own on 129th Street over to the East Side near Park Avenue. I always wanted to be the head of my apartment where nobody can make me get out. (I always said that if I wanted to buy a house, if my name can't be on there, I don't want no part of it.) I stayed at that Park Avenue place for about twenty years.

My little apartment had four small rooms, a bath, and a hallway. And it was tiny. When I lived in that little old matchbox place, I used to do all my own painting. I could almost stand in the middle of the floor and paint the sides.

And I did my own plastering too. I'd get me some plaster and mix it up. You wet the wall first with plain water and set the plaster there and smooth it down. You pat it down with a tool; then you get a rag and put water on it and make sure you get all that rough stuff off it and let it dry. Then you paint it. If you want to plaster up a hole where mice or something like that are, first you get some steel wool and put that there before you put the plaster because them mice could get through anything, but the steel wool would stop them. But I don't mess around with plumbing or electricity.

I used to paint all the time. I painted my place sometimes twice a year. I painted each room a different color: blue, pink, green—pastel colors. I always painted my kitchen yellow. I like yellow for the kitchen. I had that apartment all furnished nicely and everything. People used to come. We had fun there.

I had a dog in that apartment that I raised from a puppy. I got her from a singer friend of mine. That dog was a collie and something else. She almost looked like Lassie. There was a little hallway in the apartment and I used to put a linoleum runner down there like a rug. The dog would scratch it and bite it and I let her get by with it. I said, "She's only a dog and I love her." So I went out and bought me another runner and the dog would bite it and scratch it all up. So I went out and bought me another one and the same thing happened.

I'm gonna tell you, I will give anybody two chances but three, I will not. I took that dog and put her head right down there, where she scratched that runner up. And I beat her tail. That's what you got to do to dogs. Do you know, I didn't have any more trouble with that linoleum down there. That dog would go in the hallway but I guess she think, "Oh, no!" She might do a little scratching but she never did tear that linoleum up anymore.

I kept that dog until she was seventeen years old, then I had to put her away. When I got ready, she looked at me like to say, "How could you do it? I've been here all this time, barking, keeping people away from your door and then you gonna let them go and take me?" I cried so much that night, I tell you, you'd have thought I lost a real person. And I promised I would never get a living thing to take care of in my house again, unless it's a child. I don't want no dog. I don't want no cat. I don't want no bird. I don't even want no plant. I don't want anything like that.

I once worked for a lady that had a little dog. I made that little dog walk around on his hind legs, you know what I mean. But I really don't trust any animal. They could hurt you. Don't ever say your dog won't bite you, because you could feed that thing and when he get it in his mind to bite you when he get mad, he or she will bite.

I really did hate to move out of that apartment on Park Avenue but they said they were going to tear the building down. It wasn't torn down; it stayed empty for a long time. Then they remodeled it and it looked really nice. When they told me they were going to tear the building down, they were giving people something to give up their apartments, maybe a hundred dollars or something like that. But I moved away before they said what they were gonna do. I had a chance to move so I took it. When I heard about the apartment where I am now, I left because I said, "Money or no money, what the hell, I got to move now because it might be that I can't get in there when the time comes."

Before I left Park Avenue, I cleaned up that apartment. I want to make sure that it's clean when I move out of a place; that the windowsills, refrigerator, and everything is clean. I don't like to leave a mess anyplace even if they were gonna tear the building down. I went in there and just washed and shined the linoleum. Whoever come in, they don't even have to use it if they don't want it, but it's gonna be clean. If I leave out of this apartment where I am now, even if they make me angry— you know, like you moving because the landlord makes you angry—I would still clean up the place. If you trash the place, you're worse than the landlord 'cause if somebody do you dirt and you want to do the same to them, you are just like them.

I'm glad I'm not on Park Avenue anymore because it was so far over on the East Side. I never did like the East Side. I wouldn't move back in that neighborhood now if they would give it to me. It wasn't that it was dangerous. Every place is dangerous. People don't understand that. They say about Harlem, "Oh, you live in this environment?" I say that when somebody is ready to bother you, it doesn't matter where you are at. If you're in the wrong place at the wrong time, any place is dangerous.

When I was living on Park Avenue, everybody knew me. Some people will get angry for different little things but I never had no problem with anybody over there, not any prob-lems at all. I wasn't scared of anybody. I'd be coming in the block late at night or something like that but there'd always be somebody out there to see that I was okay. They'd say, "You all right out there, Miss Freddie Mae?" I'd say, "I'm fine." They took care of me. I knew everybody there and everybody knew me and everything like that but that wasn't the point. So when I got the chance to move to Lenox Avenue, I took it.

I've been in my building in Harlem for the last thirty-three years. It's a complex with six buildings called Lenox Ter-race, and it's like a little city in itself. It's got shops on Lenox Avenue that's part of the building. People rent them but the building owns them. They have food stores; they have tailors, they have florists, they have a drugstore but no hardware store.

I live on the twelfth floor; I think there's eighteen apart-ments on a floor. People might think the place is a project but it's not. It's owned by a private firm. And it's not a co-op; everybody rents. One time they wanted to make it a co-op but they squashed that. If it went co-op, I wouldn't buy. I don't think they would make me buy, because I'm a senior citizen.

The management paints when the time comes to paint and I hate the paint that they put on there. If you get a spot on it, it's so hard to wash off. You can mess up almost the whole wall, washing it off. I don't like that kind of thing. I like paint that you can wash if you feel like it. I really like enamel but they don't use that in my place. So what you gonna do?

I have a big old studio room. They call it a two-room suite because if you divide it, you would have two big old rooms but I don't want to divide it. There's part of my apartment I call my living room and part that I call my bedroom. It's really nice even though it's one room. It might be little but I got everything together.

Some of the apartments have a kitchen window and some have a bathroom window. I don't have a kitchen window. I just love a bathroom window because that takes everything out. In the summertime, I get more air out of that little window than I do my big windows. In the winter, you can freeze in my bathroom. That's how much wind comes through that little window. I don't have air-conditioning because I can't stand cold breezes on me. I have fans and I let the fans hit the wall, then by the time that coolness hit the wall, it kind of heats up a little bit when it comes back to me.

I made a place in the room for my terrace. Well, it's not really a terrace, but I have my furniture fixed up like a terrace, with my beach chairs so I can sit back and look out the window. I have two beach chairs, one in each corner right by the window. There's a table back there too and I got a TV sitting on that table.

Near the terrace, I made something like a picket fence with a thing you look through. I got two boxes one on each side with all kinds of plastic flowers in them. I got the same kind of flowers in each one. You know, it cost me a fortune to buy them flowers. But I kept getting them until I got exactly what I wanted. I wash the flowers and arrange them and they look so nice and pretty.

I don't like plants too much but people used to buy them for me. I had to water them and I don't want nothing like that. I don't want to be thinking about that when I go away, that somebody has to water them or they'll die. So I stop people from buying me plants. My goddaughter, Vicky, used to buy me flowers until I told her, "I don't like flowers because when they come, they're half-blooming and they bloom all of a sudden. But when I wake up the next morning, they're dead. I don't like something that's gonna die on you."

I sleep with my head to the window. I want to be looking out. I keep my blinds halfway down because there's four big huge bright lights and they shine down on me just like a flashlight. They don't have to be in my eyes at night. If I don't want them there, I can move my head. One of these days, I'm gonna find out where those lights are coming from. I'm just gonna go over there and see.

At Christmastime, I put my lights up. I have a wreath on one window and a wreath on the other. In the middle window, I have a big old wreath with Santa Claus on it. There are lights on the wreaths that go on and off; they sparkle so bright you can see them from the street twelve flights below.

I hate traveling. If I traveled, I wouldn't go far. Maybe I'd go to Washington. Or maybe I'd go to my hometown to spend a few weeks and see some of my friends that moved back there. I've taken vacations but I just don't go out of the country. I don't mind going to another city in this country but I just wouldn't want to go to another country. I think I'd have trouble getting around. I'd have trouble trying to talk.

I got a lady friend in my building. She and her husband

have really done some traveling in their life. I have got cards from those two people from all over the world. But I'm not going anyplace far like that. I don't want to find out anything about those places. I always say, "If you don't taste the steak, you ain't gonna never know how it taste."

I ain't had no money to go no place. The only place I wanted to go was Hawaii. I used to see it in the movies and I'd say, "Lord, if I ever get grown, that's where I would like to go." I always wanted to go to one of them luaus where they do the hula. Then I changed my mind because if you were going, it would either have to be by airplane or by boat. And right now, boats don't leave from New York like they used to. I remember the time when the *Rotterdam* and the *Queen Mary* used to leave from here. I went several times to see people off and I know they went from here. I saw somebody off on the *Queen Mary* twice, somebody off on the *Rotterdam* twice, and I saw somebody go off on another one. They were going overseas to different countries.

Even in this country, I wouldn't go far. One of the things I don't wish for is flying. Anything else, I might take a chance. But I will not take a chance on an airplane. You couldn't get me on an airplane with all the money in the world. It would have to be a train or bus. I should have flown on an airplane when I was young. When you're young, you're crazy. Then I wouldn't be like I am today. I wish I could make up my mind to get in one of them birds. Margaret is the one that would fly. She flew a couple of times. And my sister Victoria don't mind traveling. She'd go in a minute.

Ain't nobody gonna talk me into flying; I'll never get up there. Ain't no way in the world I'm going anyplace up in nobody's air. I'm not gonna do it unless they put the airplane down here in the street. I might even get killed on the street, but I have a better chance of crawling out if it should crack up or something like that. But there ain't no crawling out when you come from up there.

If you let me up there in that air, the airplane might say "putta-putta" like it's gonna give out or something. If it just say "putta-putta," I'd be a goner right then. Maybe they could straighten out that "putta-putta" but I wouldn't be there to see it. I would just drop dead. If something's gonna happen, they tell you. Even if the people that talk up there say, "Well, you better fasten your seat belts because we're having a little problem now" and that kind of stuff . . . Once they say that, it would just stop my heart right there. It's just as well for me to die there. But they gonna tell me nothing because I'm not gonna be up there. I'm not going on an airplane for no reason unless they kill me and want to ship me someplace. The only way you're going to get me up there is if I'm dead. And I might come back and say something to you then.

I think if I had money enough I would go on a cruise and have my own cabin, like have my own quarters. I wouldn't mind going on a boat, like I could do my stuff in there, like cook or whatever. Anything could happen on a boat, but I could grab hold of something or whatever and I might live. In case something happens, who knows, maybe somebody could fish me out. But I'm thinking on an airplane—if I come down from up there—there is no chance. When I'm coming down in that airplane, I'd be dead before I hit the ground anyway.

I don't want to be tricked into anything. Somebody might want you to go so bad, they might give you a pill or something to knock you out there for a while and put you in there. Then when you wake up, you are up there. If I wake up and find out I'm flying, whoever it was that nailed me is gonna be a dead duck 'cause I'm gonna start pumping them and hitting them. By the time somebody gets me, they're not gonna be alive. I'm gonna get rid of them, so help me. I don't want them messing up my mind.

Even if I don't go up in the air, I might get killed by an airplane. Where my house is sitting is the runway for airplanes going over to La Guardia or Kennedy airports. When they come through Harlem, they ain't got too far to go. Once they cross over the East River, they're there anyway. I can lay up in my bed and see the airplanes coming straight over my house. Sometimes they're pretty high but sometimes they can be very low. When they come through my place, they are so low that they are big, big, big. Believe it when I tell you.

Right around the corner from me in my building, people sit on their terrace and they can wave at the people in the airplane 'cause it's flying so low. One of them suckers could decide to fall and it could be on my house. You never know. I still could get killed by an airplane even though I ain't never been in one. So I might as well stay here and let it kill me on the ground.

Things are different now that I've retired. When I was working, I never got to work until round about ten, so I'd get up at eight o'clock. I always ate breakfast before I left and I never wanted to go out of the house without the bed being made.

Now when I wake up in the morning, I get up about seven-thirty. I don't ever jump right out of bed unless the doorbell or the telephone rings. I sit on the bed for a minute or two and then I get up, go out, and get my newspaper. I just put something on because I know I'm coming back in. I just hope that I don't get knocked down by a car with my pajamas underneath my clothes. I come out every morning at about seven-thirty, hot or cold. Even when it's raining, even when it's snowing—I don't care what it is—I'm out there. The air is much cleaner in the morning because there ain't nothing running to make any dust or anything. I gets out and catches it; I take a deep breath.

I see everybody going to work but I'm out there too, getting the newspaper. People can set their clocks by me. Everybody looks out for me when I get the paper; the cars come out of the yard and the people are waving out of the cars. Everybody's waving, waving, waving.

I get my paper and other people's papers. A lady on the first floor once asked me to get her a paper. I said, "I go out every day. Would you like for me to bring you the paper every day?" They give me the money for the paper—whatever their papers will cost for the week. Then when the week is out, they give it to me again. Every Christmas, they give me a nice envelope. I don't want them to do that, 'cause I'm gonna get my paper anyway, but every Christmas they do.

I take my bath at night where I can be in the house afterward. (A bath in the morning might give you a cold.) If I take a bath in the daytime and go out—I don't care if it's the Fourth of July—I'll catch a cold. About eight years ago, I went home for a family reunion. And I didn't want people down there to say, "She got up this morning and she didn't even take a bath." So I went in and took me a good bath in the morning and the sun was hot as fire down there. Then I went out with short sleeves and before I left from down there, I had a cold.

I never did like showers. Even when I was sleeping-in the people's houses and they had a shower in my room, I still would go in their bathroom and take my bath. I want to get in the tub and let that hot water run down my back and around my neck. I just dip in there, scoop it up, and put it all over my face. One of my friends says he takes a bath first and then he takes a shower. I said, "Well, that's your little red wagon." I always say, "To each his own, as long as you're clean."

Ivory soap is what I take a bath in. I don't like all that perfumed soap. Ivory soap is not sweet; it's just clean. It smells clean. After I have my bath, I put Vaseline on my face. It keeps my skin nice and moist. That's the only thing that goes on my face. I don't want it to get messed up. Vaseline goes on my whole body, even on my feet. My feet ain't all crusted up like some people's. Some people have to scrape on themselves, you know what I mean? I just don't want to get ashy.

When I come back in from getting the paper, I make my bed. Then I brush my teeth and get myself cleaned up a little. I run my sink full of water and I get myself a sponge, wash all over with soap, and I rinse myself off. The only thing I use for my hair is a grease called Royal Crown. It makes my hair shiny and then I brush it.

I'll put a little perfume on. I don't use cologne. When I worked for Miss Hansen, she'd give me a little bottle of Chanel No. 5 every birthday, every Christmas. She was writing about those things and they would send the stuff to her. It was expensive but she would give it to me. That's how I got stuck on French perfumes. When she stopped working, she didn't get it anymore. She told me, "Freddie Mae, I know you like that and I would love very much to continue giving it to you but it's very expensive." She showed me in the book how much it cost and everything. I said, "I can't afford no Chanel No. 5." So I just attached myself to perfume that had the word "French" up there on the label. It could cost five dollars, ten dollars, twenty dollars. Whatever it cost and if it was made by French people, I would buy it. When you read on the bottle, it tells you there, "Made by the French," so you know that it's French perfume.

I have the water on for my coffee and I leave it boiling but I don't even start my breakfast. I have to read the paper first because I don't want to wolf my breakfast down. I spend about half an hour in the morning reading the paper, maybe a little more, because I want to know what's going on. I read every page of the paper, from front to back, about how somebody done kill or somebody done rob or somebody done rape.

I read Ann Landers, Dr. Brothers, the funnies; sometimes I read the recipes, but I don't bother with that too much because I know how to cook and I don't need to know what somebody else is cooking.

I'm at the point now where I mostly look to see stories about murder cases. I like to know who it is and where it happened, whether it's a man or a woman and who did the murder, a child or a grown-up. But something like that ain't in there every day. Thank the Lord, somebody doesn't murder somebody every day.

. . .

I've been reading about the bombings of the black churches down South. I don't know who's doing it, and I really would like to know what is the reason to bomb a church? People are so cruel today. All that energy that they have, they use it to make up these bombs. If they would put it to good use, they wouldn't need to bomb nothing. They'd have more money and more leverage. They would have more everything if they'd take up the time they're using to do those dirty things. They would have more time for themselves and their families. But these are sick people. They are sick and they are killing us. I don't mean just blacks. They are killing everybody 'cause they're sick. Then when they catch them, the parents will say, "Well, he's a little bit off." Or "He's been a little this or a little that." But why couldn't they think he was a little off before he did that? That's what I can't understand.

After I read the paper, I have my breakfast. Sometimes I have two eggs, bacon or sausage. Sometimes I'll eat hominy grits with it, sometimes it'll be toast, and I always have a glass of fresh orange juice, from two oranges that I squeeze every morning. And I take my vitamins, One-A-Day. I've been taking them so long that I can't say whether the doctor told me to take them or I just started taking them. And they seem to be doing all right for me. I'm still going.

I eat three meals a day and I don't eat in between. Let's say I eat my breakfast around eight-thirty, then by two o'clock I'll eat my lunch. I eat my big meal at night. I'll eat my dinner about seven-thirty or a quarter to eight. And that's it. No in-betweens. Like you get up and say, "I done ate but I think I'll get me another sandwich." I have my three meals and that's it. If I want dessert, that's the only in-between I eat. I could have eaten it with the meal if I had wanted to but I make sure that's all I have after the meal. I drink coffee in the morning and that's the only hot liquid I drink on and on, unless I have some soup for lunch or dinner. For lunch, I drink ginger ale. For my dinner, sometimes I drink ginger ale, sometimes I drink water. I like iced tea in the summertime but I haven't had it for quite a spell. I used to share lunch with a girlfriend, but she moved away. Since I've been by myself, I don't make iced tea or lemonade anymore.

Around nine-thirty or so in the morning, I take me a walk, most of the time around 125th Street, which is about seven, eight, nine blocks from me. You know, that's a good ways. Then I walk from there over to Seventh Avenue and I come down Seventh Avenue and I go to 135th Street. That's a busy street where everybody's hanging around. I do that every day. I will stay out about 45 minutes, and walk about twenty-five blocks. I don't ever go the same way. I don't care where you're going, even if you're going to work, don't ever go the same way, because it's not good. If somebody is meaning to harm you or wants to harm you or something, they can say, "Oh, she passes down here every day." I say, "Always mix it up, even if you have to get off the bus and walk a couple of blocks." Some people might wonder why I do it like that, but that's my business.

When I come back from my walk, if I feel like I want to do a little something around the house—dusting or something like that—I'll do it. If I don't feel like doing it, I don't do it. Whatever I got to do, I always do it in the morning. If I got to go shopping, I do it in the morning. All my telephone calls, I do them in the morning.

Round about twelve-thirty, I watch my soaps. That was something I always did want to do when I was working, but I never did. I used to say, "If I ever retire, I'm going to watch my soaps at home and nobody's gonna bother me." So now I sit up there and watch my soaps between twelve-thirty and four o'clock. And if I'm watching, I don't want nobody to bother me. I didn't use to answer my phone when the soaps were on. But now I have too many sick people in the family for me not to answer when the phone rings.

I like everything about the soaps. I call them my house family. I know who I like and who I would like to like. Some of the subjects I don't care for and I might go in the kitchen and do something else but I can still hear them talking. One big reason I like them is that the people there have more problems than I'm having.

Something is always happening in the soaps. They don't keep it on one thing all the time. You see about five or six different stories in one soap. They'll be on this here doing something and then when they come back another time, they're someplace else doing something else, and then the commercial comes and when they come back again, it's doing something else. You are up and down all the time in those soaps. But I just love 'em, love 'em, love 'em.

If I miss anything, I got a girlfriend who calls me when I get home, and tells me everything, almost like I'm sitting there, watching it myself. She even tells me which way the girl's hair was blowing when she and her boyfriend got in the car. She tells me everything so I don't have to worry about missing it.

Lots of men watch the soaps too. I got a man friend who will call me and we'll be fussing and fussing about who we think did this and who we think did that. He'll have what he thinks and I'll have what I think.

Sometimes I think the people on the soaps are very stupid. I didn't want one girl to take the man of another girl. It wasn't fair. She had a man ready to marry her and she done quit that man to take the man that the other girl got. I was so mad about that. My friends, they get mad at me. They say that this girl deserves what happens. I say, "I don't care what she is. I don't think the other girl should've taken her man. Why she want to take the man when they have men out there wanting her?"

I don't waste my eyes with other stuff on TV. Not that something is wrong with my eyes, but I'm not going to hurt them by watching TV night and day. And I don't listen to the radio too much at night. Sometimes I just read a book or a magazine.

All Saturday and Sunday, I don't watch no TV at all. I save my eyes for Monday. On Saturdays and Sundays, there's no TV at my house unless there's somebody else coming who wants to watch it. If somebody comes to visit and they want to watch it, I just go someplace else in the apartment.

I listen to jazz on the radio, all through the afternoon when I'm home on Saturday and Sunday. It's playing all those pieces that I used to dance to in the forties, the fifties, and the sixties. I listen to the same station all the time, because it's one that gives me all the old pieces from back when I was really getting down, when I was really dancing. That gets me going. Sometimes I'll stop what I'm doing and I'll dance.

I can sit up now and put on my radio and it plays the music of all them people that's dead. And I just sit back and I can see myself dancing. I dance a lot in the house. You might ask me, "How can you clap and dance by yourself?" Well, I can do it with people and I can do it without. Other people aren't feeling the music like I'm feeling it. If they're there, I'm going to feel it and if they're not there, I'm still gonna feel it. So why can't I dance? If I get where I couldn't hear music, I really don't know what would happen.

Sometimes I'll be sleeping and if a piece comes on that I really like, I get out of bed in the middle of the night. I got my nightclothes on and everything but I get up and dance.

I don't see many movies because I'm not going to ruin my eyes on them, but every once in a blue moon, I go to the movies. Movies today don't have too much of what we used to see years ago: Bette Davis, Joan Crawford, Lena Horne, Elizabeth Taylor. I thought that Lena Horne was the prettiest colored woman in the world. When I was coming up, I tried to put her like my pinup girl. She's still pretty even though she's an old woman.

Years ago movies were about people who love each other. Today, if you see a love picture, they don't make no money off it. I can't understand it. They want to cut somebody's neck off or blow up things. That's what got a whole lot of kids doing things that maybe they wouldn't really do.

When I was a kid, they showed Westerns most of the time. I would sit up in there and I carried on so bad. Like if somebody shoot somebody in the movie and go around into another room and then somebody else come in, I'd say, "Don't you know, he went around there." I'd say, "He went behind! He's right under there!" I was old enough not to do it, but I'd shout out, "Shoot him! Shoot him!" The other people sitting there didn't hush me. They would move. And I'd look around and I'd have a whole section of that movie theater all to myself.

And later on they made those third-dimension movies where you put on little glasses to see them. One time I had on those little glasses and one of the tigers jumped and he jumped right in my lap. Those glasses made that happen. I started to holler. I tried to get away from him. You should have seen me fight. I took those glasses off and I went home. I'll really never forget that 3-D. That tiger jumped right in my lap, so help me God!

At night, before I go to sleep, I say my prayers and tell the good Lord that I love Him and I pray for all of my friends and my country. I sleep so good. I figure that when you're sleeping all night long, you got to be dead. I love getting up in the morning after I done died all night long. I be so glad to get up.

I'm always on time. My brother Julius says, "Freddie Mae, you shouldn't look for everybody to be like you." I say, "That's not the point. If somebody's a certain way, they think you supposed to be that certain way too." But I don't think people should be like that. If someone was supposed to pick me up, I would wait about 45 minutes. I think that's fair because you know trains or buses or whatever you coming on can be a little late. If you're not there after that 45 minutes, I'm either going back home or going wherever we supposed to be going. That's the way I would do it. You teach a child about being on time but I don't think you should have to teach a grown-up. We are grown. We should already know.

I take care of my bills before I do anything else. The first of the month everything goes out for me 'cause I want to have a whole 'nother month to get it together. Everything is paid up for that month so I can have the whole month to think about it again. I learned that from a lady I was working for and I've never forgotten it. I used to be there with that lady when she was making out her checks for different things: her rent, her groceries, her children, whatever. I just always was with her.

I pay all my bills in person, and with cash money. I pay them by money order. I always go to the check-cashing place across the street from me. I don't have a checking account. I never wrote out a check for myself. I wrote out a check for other people and let them sign it but I never wrote out a check for myself.

Somebody told me one time, "Freddie, you might not be able to get it for the first of the month and they'll be looking for you to pay it the first of the month." I said, "If that day comes, then I'll have to work it out a different way." I only do what I can do. I hope it don't get where I won't be able to pay on the first of the month, I really do, because that's my thing and it would hurt me very bad.

I was twenty-one years old when I started voting. I vote every time there's a vote, even in the primaries. Any time that you're being put up there that you got to vote, I go. Even if the people can't win, I still go and put my name down. I'm a

Democrat all the way. I don't cross the line. If they don't win, they just don't win, but I vote for them anyway.

The people I worked for, they used to want to know who I was going to vote for. I said, "Now, wait a minute. Do I look stupid? I'm not going to tell you who I vote for. I know you won't tell me who you vote for." And I never did tell anybody. All I could tell them is that I'm a Democrat. I said, "You can take anything you want from that, but I won't tell you how I'm gonna vote. That's my business." If people wanted you to know, they'd just let the voting be out in the open and let everybody see what you push. But that's your private business. You could get in there, in the booth, and change your mind.

Years ago, all that Southern people used to think about was going in the field, picking cotton, going to school, and games in the schoolyard. There was nothing much to talk about. Sure, the girls would talk about the boys and the boys would talk about the girls. But years ago, my people didn't tell any jokes.

I really know some jokes now. I don't make them up myself, I learned them from people. In the years of coming up North. I declare I know about three hundred of them now.

I don't forget jokes, for some reason. All a person got to do is tell me one time. I don't have to write it down. I can come home and tell it to somebody else, and I can make that same joke go all the way to Florida on the telephone.

I always have to have a little fun. When I go to Atlantic City on the bus, I look out the window and see a stretch limousine. I jump right up, point out the window, and say, "Didn't I tell you not to take that car out of the garage? I told you not to take it." I'm looking out the window and talking to that stretch limousine and everybody on the bus gets a kick out of it.

I prefer telling my jokes around my own people because most of them are about my people. It would be cruel if I told them outside my race. You would have to be on the ball to understand what I'm talking about, so maybe it wouldn't tickle you. Like our people are mostly on the ball; they laugh at things. They understand what you're talking about. The jokes that I tell, they're only for grown-ups. Some of the jokes are filthy, you know what I mean? Filthy. If you heard me, you would swear that I was one of the nastiest people in the world. I don't like to be around kids when I tell them. I don't want the kids to say, "That old lady who told that joke is such a so-and-so-and-so."

I can tell a long joke but I will never tell it long. I make all my jokes short. I will cut them in half every time. Some people will say, "This man, he went all the way around in Brooklyn and he came back to Staten Island and then he went all around there." They tell it long-long. By the time they're finished, you don't want to laugh.

Sometimes I really laugh to myself. I think about something and I laugh. If I get tickled, I'm gonna laugh. It might sound crazy but I don't care. If I get tickled, I'll laugh in a church. You know if you gonna laugh, you can cover your mouth but it still gonna come out. You can't hide your tickledness. And when I get tickled, I get tickled. Who cares what you think about me? That's your problem. I'll fall down if it's funny enough. I get so tickled, I'll fall down on the floor.

I like to play cards. When we have our card games, we ain't got time for serious stuff. Nobody don't come out with nothing that could be very important or serious. None of that stuff like, "Oh, So-and-so died." Nobody wants to talk about things like that in our card game. It's always something funny. We only tell jokes.

But we don't have too much time to tell jokes because you don't take but a little while to deal out the cards. Then you got to pick your cards up and try to find out what you got. Once in a while, though, I'll jump in and tell a joke to make somebody laugh: I don't think the others know quite as many stories as I know.

Then we play another hand and somebody else will say something and we're all laughing together. When I was working, I used to leave from my job and sometimes I'd be so tired and frustrated. I knew that if I could get to that card table, then I could go and do another day's work. If you got a problem on your mind, it will still be there, but you don't think about it if you're laughing and telling jokes.

Me and a lady I be knowing for fifty years were talking about putting a group together to play cards. We said we could get some girls and have something to do because you can't be hanging out in the street no more. We're getting too old for that. For about two years, we kept trying to get this thing together. We finally got five people, a small group, but that means we can all sit up to one table.

In our group now we have a subway worker, a retired nurse, a nurse who's still working, a hairdresser, and then we have me. We tell jokes but we don't talk about people's lives in the group. I don't ask questions so I don't know if they're married or not; I don't discuss their love lives. One of the girls, she talks a lot about the fellas, but I don't think you should bring them in there. When I get busy, I want to play cards. And we ain't got no time to talk about kids. We ain't got that kind of time. What you want to talk about kids for anyway? Ain't you playing cards? I think the oldest one in our group is a woman who's over seventy-five, but that's not old if you still got your faculties up there. Boy, that woman can play some cards! For being old people, we really do have a good time.

Games give us old people something to do without going to the senior centers. I'm not going to the centers. I have too many outside friends that we can do things together. When people go to them centers like that, maybe they don't have anybody. I know people that go there to eat. Some of them have breakfast and all that kind of stuff, but I don't want to go there. I want to be with my friends.

One week the card game's in your house, then next week, in someone else's. We call it round house. And we got it so nobody has to cook. We only eat snacks like potato chips and popcorn. Then we get some cold cuts. The last time I bought some beef baloney and turkey baloney and I cut it up in beautiful little squares.

We play for money in each other's houses. Everybody puts a certain amount of money in the pot. And whoever's house we're playing in gets a quarter out of that pot. That's your cut.

Each person lays out about ten dollars and may the best man win. Sometimes you lose your ten; sometimes they lose theirs. Sometimes you come out ahead. Sometimes you come out broke. But you just have to be a good sport. Some people say that playing cards takes skill, but you just have to be lucky. I know there are people who win because they cheat. But if you're gonna play a decent game, you just play.

We play on Sundays. Some of them go to church but we play after church. We don't start until one-thirty. And they don't have to worry about me, because I don't go to church. One of the ladies in the group sang in the choir but that ain't got nothing to do with having fun. God wants you to have fun. That's why he put us here.

People are not like me. I'm very different from other people. I'm gonna say it for myself. I don't know why I am that way. I wouldn't do what other people did. I don't eat like nobody. I don't drink like nobody. I have my own mind. It's not that I was well educated, but I have my own mind. You know your mind is yours. You can't learn that in school. You got to think for yourself. That's the way I've always been. I do show off sometimes but I don't see why I shouldn't do that every once in a while.

I heard a saying that crazy people survive. And somebody else could go in there and have all the sense in the world and not survive. I'm the seventh child, so I know I'm lucky. But I also might be crazy. So if I'm crazy, I'm gonna stay crazy. 'Cause that's the way I am and I cannot change from what I been through all my life. Let me stay here; I'm doing all right just as I am. Some people hate to tell their age but I will yell it. I was coming out of my house the other day and a fella said, "You walk like a teenager." I told him, "I am."

Sometimes when I see people my age I have to shake my head. They just sit. They can keep up with me in talking but when it comes to doing things, they could be bashful. Let's say some music would get out there. Some of my friends would just stand but I'd start dancing.

I live by myself but I can have fun because I know how to entertain myself. And I'm really glad I'm old. Every day, I learn something. Even if I'm out there in the street, every day I learn something different. Some people know a lot by reading, but I experienced life. Knowing is different than reading. You know more about it than you would know if you only read about it. Don't get me wrong; I think you should read too. But when you experience something, that means a lot to you.

I don't regret a thing through my life, when I had and when I didn't have. Whatever I did, I always tried to make fun for myself with it. I like happiness and I'm happy most of the time. It don't take much to make me happy. Little things make me happy. I don't cry, you know. The only time I cry is if I'm happy. And if I'm in a place where I can't be happy, I won't stay there.

I never wanted to be under somebody's thumb. Nothing beats being your own boss. I can't let somebody control me. I don't want to get myself so deep in anything that I can't pull out. Nobody can hold me. I ain't got nothing but that's just the way I am.

All my life, I've been doing, you know, just doing. Now that I'm not working, I just want to do what I want to do, not something that I *got* to do. I just want to keep the rest of my little life to just enjoy me. I want to be free. I want to go when I want to go. I want to come when I want to come. I think I've paid my dues.

I'm a kisser, I'm a joke teller, I'm a dancer. I'm a somewhat everything and nothing big. I'm not a stuck-up. I don't have none of that thinking that you're better than anybody. I didn't go to college. I didn't have no big great job. I haven't had anything big. I was just down-to-earth and I got along fine. I'm my own person, that's what it is, and I'm still moving. If I slow down, if I just stop getting around, you know, maybe I could tell you something else.

BLACK ICE

by Lorene Cary

Black Ice is Lorene Cary's story of her life as a bright, ambitious black teenager from Philadelphia who, when transplanted to an elite school in New Hampshire, becomes a scholarship student determined to succeed without selling out. In recounting her journey into selfhood, Cary creates a universally recognizable document of a woman's adolescence.

Memoir/0-679-73745-6

IN HER OWN WORDS

Women's Memoirs from Australia,
New Zealand, Canada, and the United States

edited and with an introduction by Jill Ker Conway

A revealing distillation of women's experience from the British Commonwealth world from which Jill Ker Conway came compared with women's lives in the United States, which is now her home. Conway explores how the worlds of politics and the private intersect in four offshoots of the old British world and how women have made a difference—with their honesty and the scale of their struggle for self-knowledge and autonomy, and by the power of their writing.

Biography/0-679-78153-6

HAVANA DREAMS

by Wendy Gimbel

A fascinating, powerfully evocative story of four generations of Cuban women, through whose lives the author illuminates a vivid picture—both personal and historical—of Cuba in our century. "When I want to read a culture," writes Wendy Gimbel in her prologue, "I listen to stories about families, sensing in their contours the substance of larger mysteries." And certainly in the Revuelta family she has found a source of both mystery and revelation.

Biography/0-679-75070-3

THINKING IN PICTURES
by Temple Grandin

In this unprecedented book, Grandin writes from the dual perspectives of a scientist and an autistic person. She tells us how she managed to breach the boundaries of autism to function in the outside world. What emerges is the document of an extraordinary human being, one who gracefully bridges the gulf between her condition and our own while shedding light on our common identity.

Memoir/0-679-77289-8

A SCHOOLTEACHER IN OLD ALASKA
The Story of Hannah Breece
by Jane Jacobs

Jane Jacobs, Hannah Breece's great-niece, here offers an historical context to Breece's remarkable eyewitness account of life in turn-of-the-century Alaska. A powerful work of women's history that provides important—and, at times, unsettling—insights into the unexamined assumptions and attitudes that governed white settlers' behavior toward native communities in the earliest days of the twentieth century.

Biography/0-679-77633-8

THE LADIES' GALLERY
by Irene Vilar

Irene Vilar, granddaughter of Lolita Lebrón, the revered martyr for Puerto Rican independence who in 1954 sprayed the U. S. House of Representatives with gunfire revisits the legacy of her grandmother and that of her anguished mother, who leapt from a speeding car when Vilar was eight. Eleven years after her mother's death, Vilar awakens in a psychiatric hospital and begins to face the devastating inheritance of abandonment and suicide passed down to her from grandmother and mother.

Memoir/0-679-74546-7